THE QUEERING
OF THE
AMERICAN CHILD

THE QUEERING OF THE AMERICAN CHILD

How a New School Religious Cult Poisons the Minds and Bodies of Normal Kids

LOGAN LANCING
WITH JAMES LINDSAY

🧠 New Discourses

First edition: February 2024

Cover copyright © 2024 New Discourses, LLC.

Hardcover ISBN: 979-8-9897416-0-1
Paperback ISBN: 979-8-9897416-9-4
eBook ISBN: 979-8-9897416-1-8

Imprint: Independently published

Published by New Discourses, LLC.
Orlando, Florida
https://newdiscourses.com

*For the parents searching for answers and
the people speaking the truth, no matter the cost*

CONTENTS

ADVANCE PRAISE FOR
THE QUEERING OF THE AMERICAN CHILD

"Queer Theory is the distillation of the most toxic intellectual poisons of our age. If it were just the personal philosophy of a few eccentrics, we could ignore it. But, as Logan Lancing and James Lindsay show, it has all the marks of a cult whose adherents have access to most of our children—from inner-city public schools to the most expensive prep schools. If we want to defeat this cult and protect the next generation, we must inoculate our children against it. *The Queering of the American Child* will give you the medicine to do that. Read this book and take its lessons to heart—before it's too late."

—**Jay Richards,** Ph.D., Director, Richard and Helen DeVos Center for Life, Religion, and Family and the William E. Simon Senior Research Fellow in American Principles and Public Policy at the Heritage Foundation

"As someone who regrets being trans, I wish I had read this book before I went through the surgery and hormones. If I had understood how queer theory functions as a religious cult, I wouldn't have thought transition was a safe or effective way to treat my mental health issues."

—**Laura Becker,** speaker, writer, detransitioner

"Lancing and Lindsay deftly expose the philosophy that pushes the indoctrination of children, and the separation of children from parents, in this terrifying but deeply necessary new book."

—**Karol Markowicz,** columnist for the *New York Post* and Fox News, born in the USSR

"Even as someone who is quite aware of what is happening, this book was still eye opening for me. I swear, if everyone read this book, the whole trans debate would end instantly."
—**Pamela Garfield-Jaeger,** LCSW, anti-Woke clinical social worker and author

"*The Queering of the American Child* is a compelling must-read for every person scratching their head and wondering what on earth has happened to society in recent years. This book provides an incisive account of the devastating influence of Queer Theory both within pedagogy and psychology. If you want to understand Queer Theory and how it impacts, read this book."
—**Stella O'Malley,** Psychotherapist, writer, president of Genspect

"I really think this is an extremely important book. The Christian community is totally ignorant of the things it addresses. This book meets the need of the hour. If you have a pulse, you need to read this book."
—**Rev. Andy Woodard,** Pastor, Providence Reformed Baptist Church, NY, NY

"*The Queering of the American Child* is one of the most honest, candid, and blunt treatments of the Queer Theory movement you will ever come across. With unmitigated courage and conviction, Lancing and Lindsay audaciously exposit the diabolical tenets that comprise the Queer Theory agenda in a way that leaves no ambiguity as to its injurious aims and designs for society's children."
—**Darrell B. Harrison,** member of the pastoral staff at Redeemer Bible Church in Gilbert, Arizona, and cohost of the *Just Thinking* podcast

"Lancing's *Queering of the American Child* explains the genesis of queer theory and queer activism and how it has infiltrated so many institutions, from government, to our courts, and perhaps most worrisome, into the classrooms of our youth. His well sourced book should be a wake-up call to us all as this theory and their activists see queering our children as their moral duty, and will not rest until they've succeeded."

—**Jennifer Lahl,** filmmaker and Founder, Center for Bioethics & Culture Network

"The parallels discussed in this book between what's happening in today's schools and Marxists influenced writings from the past are made so clear and comprehensive. Everyone who wants to understand how we got here needs to read this book."

—**Jessica Graham,** Programs Director, Moms for Liberty

"*The Queering of the American Child* is a book that needed to be written because the issues at stake are crucial ones. The authors have done their work well. Every parent, educator, and administrator needs to carefully consider what this book presents."

—**Michael O'Fallon,** founder of Sovereign Nations

"*The Queering of the American Child* is the most powerful and devastating examination to date of the dangerous cult that is brainwashing, recruiting, and mutilating American children by the millions. The evil agenda is laid bare on every page, along with the facts and evidence needed for parents and taxpayers to stop this monstrous movement in its tracks."

—**Alex Newman,** journalist, educator, author of *Indoctrinating Our Children to Death*

"Like getting a cancer diagnosis, this book is terrifyingly necessary. Queer activism is a fast-moving, widespread disease in the American school system. Unless it is decisively exposed and radiated, it will infect our kids and grandkids with devastating effects that will last for generations. This book is the radiation the whole system needs. No matter who you are, you need what it says. Give it to administrators and school board members. I hope it has the widest possible reading. The stakes are that high!"
—**Dr. Jon Benzinger,** Lead Pastor, Redeemer Bible Church in Gilbert, Arizona

"I just finished reading the book, *The Queering of the American Child,* and it is AMAZING! I feel like all of these bits and pieces of knowledge I have were put together to complete a puzzle. The more I learn, the more I am determined to fight this battle for our children, and reading this book fueled that fire even more."
—**Janice Danforth,** Moms for Liberty chapter chair, Tulsa County, OK

"The cult of Queer Theory cannot be opposed without a clear eyed understanding of its origins, aims, and manners of manipulation. *The Queering of the American Child* lays bare all of the above and brings great clarity to a topic known for being intentionally bewildering. Lancing and Lindsay have done us a great service in doing their homework and carefully sifting through reams of Queer Theory literature. The result is a fascinating, illuminating, and seminal read."
—**Noelle Mering,** author of *Awake, Not Woke*

INTRODUCTION

American education is in the grip of a religious cult. What started in the 1990s as a small group of abnormal, weird, and deviant disciples has since ballooned into a tremendous political force in our schools. This cult preaches a new religion of sex, "gender," and sexuality, and they use school policy and teaching practices to brainwash children into their poisonous doctrine. This cult has long known that classrooms are fertile recruiting grounds with soft, vulnerable targets. Today, children across America find themselves under the spell of *Queer Theory*.

Queer Theory is based on the mystical religious teachings of Michel Foucault, Judith Butler, Eve Kosofsky Sedgwick, Deborah P. Britzman, and many *others*. These *Queer Theorists* created the Queer Theory gospels that cultists worldwide now draw upon to push children to destabilize tradition, eliminate social norms, and poison their minds and bodies. Queer Theory is the revealed knowledge that motivates thousands of kids to wield political activism against society and themselves. Children influenced by Queer Theory adopt new "gender identities," fantasize about "social transitioning," perform drag, and experiment with fictional sexualities and related behaviors.

The leaders of this cult—the *inner circle*—spend much of

their time directing the cult's bleeding-edge secrets, plans, and strategies. This group doesn't believe in all aspects of cult doctrine, but they know they can use the cult strategically to achieve their ultimate goal—power. The inner circle wields the cult's tremendous monetary and cultural power to finance and influence cult activism and expansion. The inner circle is home to the leaders of global organizations, universities, industries, and governments.

Surrounding the inner circle of the cult are groups of "awakened" scholars and activists who form the cult's *inner school*. The inner school is home to activist academics, organizations, subject-matter experts, teachers, consultants, and policymakers who have undergone cult initiation and are familiar with the cult's teachings and practices. They are the cult's *true believers* in most cases or, in some others, opportunistic players who know the cult's doctrine thoroughly and use it to advance their own social, political, and material interests. Those in Queer Theory's inner school are called *Queer Activists*.

Queer Activists advance cult doctrine by studying the gospels of the cult and by conditioning the beliefs and behaviors of lower cult members and potential initiates. Queer Activists in the inner school "do the work" of meeting the inner circle's demands. Queer Activists are wholly committed to the cult and have mostly severed ties with anyone who doesn't share their faith. The inner school's cult attachment is both intellectual and emotional, and its members are fiercely loyal to the teachings and prescriptions of the cult doctrine, Queer Theory, with which they are considerably familiar. The inner school Queer Activists defend the cult at all costs.

The largest layer of the cult is home to initiates—the *outer school*. The people in the outer school are drawn to the cult because it offers them enlightenment and a path to salvation.

Their ties to the cult are overwhelmingly social and emotional. In fact, these cult initiates are mostly unaware of the cult's deeper doctrine and goals and in many cases only know little of the doctrine except at the surface level. In most cases, cult initiates have never read any of the cult's gospels and have no idea what the cult's obvious or hidden goals are. On the other hand, their friends are in the cult and think it's what it means to be a *good person*. Their initiated friends create a social circle that defines "inclusion" in terms of accepting and promoting the cult's doctrine. The outer school is home to those who have been deceived by the cult's manipulation, propaganda, and activism. The initiates of the outer school are the cult's primary victims and serve as cash cows, foot soldiers, sacrifices, and, depending on the person, potential inner-school converts.

Like all cult recruiters, Queer Activists use emotionally manipulative methods to control cult members and recruit new outer school initiates. For instance, the cult "love bombs" potential recruits with affection and praise. Queer Activists welcome recruits into a "safe" and "inclusive" environment where they feel like they are the most important people in the world and in which they are protected from ideas that might challenge cult doctrine, something experts in cult psychology call *milieu control*. The cult preys on the confused, vulnerable, and disenfranchised with a siren's call of total affirmation. Initiates in the outer school feel *euphoric* when they find the cult—a feeling that is typical of stepping into any cult, at least initially. Queer Activists offer them solutions to resolve all of their confusion, alienation, loneliness, and pain, an affirming social environment, and something to do that feels meaningful and productive.

Love-bombing is part of the "positive" part of a cyclical process of abuse during cult initiation. The negative part of the cycle involves deliberately inducing trauma to create conditions of vulnerability, embarrassment, and even humiliation. Taken together, this cycle of abuse is called *trauma bonding*, and Queer Activists skillfully deploy it as a mechanism to initiate and control cult members.

Trauma bonding involves exposing children to age-inappropriate content related to sex, "gender," and sexuality, causing deep psychological disturbances. These disturbances generate emotions that are difficult to cope with, especially for innocent children who aren't yet equipped to deal with such topics, especially on fraudulent terms. Once disturbed, children search for affirmation, "healing," kindness, and love. They find their relief in the very hands that have just abused them. Cults have long used this tactic to foster a growing state of social and emotional dependency among their targets.

The cycle of abuse and relief found in trauma bonding serves multiple purposes within the cult's structure. Firstly, it solidifies the hierarchical control, with Queer Activists exerting authority over cult initiates. By subjecting initiates to this cycle of trauma and relief, Queer Activists reinforce the cult doctrine of Queer Theory under conditions of isolation and dependency. This environment is ripe for conducting initiations and rites, often discreetly executed in after-school clubs tailored for this very indoctrination. These practices not only deepen the commitment of the initiates but also ensure their indoctrination into the cult's core beliefs and values. Furthermore, the cyclical nature of this abuse aids in maintaining secrecy within the cult. Children don't want to rat out their abusers when those very abusers make them feel "included" and "loved for who they really are."

As initiates become more deeply involved, the secrecy

surrounding these practices grows, creating a barrier against external scrutiny and criticism. The emotional rollercoaster of trauma bonding also reinforces loyalty as initiates, craving relief and acceptance, become more tightly bound to the cult's ideology and community. In this way, Queer Activists not only control their current members but also effectively recruit new ones, preying on their vulnerabilities and offering them a seemingly supportive and affirming environment. The euphoria that new initiates experience upon joining the cult is a typical, yet misleading, allure of such abusive systems, disguising the deeper, more insidious layers of manipulation and control at play. As we will see later, Queer Activists deliberately and knowingly engage in this process by inducing and resolving personal identity crises in children through the process of *Queer Education*.

What the cult offers its initiates is a subscription to endless "work" on behalf of the cult, primarily in engaging in its core activities and recruiting new members. Some of *the work* Queer Activists offer is social activism, which faces outward, though much of it is inward-facing work of personal transformation. The inner work transforms its victims into Queer cultists—people who *identify as* avatars of the cult doctrine. The outer work solidifies the social environment of the cult and strengthens commitment to the cult while spreading it to others. Strict social expectations with powerful social and emotional rewards (affirmation, celebration, belonging) and punishments (criticism, problematizing, struggle) are tied to both the inner and outer cult work.

When the cult can't find vulnerable people to bolster recruitment, it creates them. The cult is very good at convincing ordinary people that society has mistreated and abandoned them—or will if they confess any of their personal secrets, questions, or doubts. Queer Activists use fear-mongering to convince people that various aspects of their biology, personality, habits, and interests are relentlessly attacked by mostly invisible forces hidden in language and the "common sense" of day-to-day life. They teach their victims that the world will reject them for aspects of who they are, but the cult will accept, affirm, and celebrate them. Queer Activists train people to be vulnerable by teaching them to look for oppression in *everything*. In this way, Queer Theory sells both a problem and the solution to that problem. The cult is obsessed with the logic of the circle.

Once in the cult, Queer Activists use abusive techniques to condition cult attitudes, beliefs, and behaviors. Peer pressure, guilt-tripping, gaslighting, and the constant threat of punishment keep the cult in check, on message, and to the task. The messaging relentlessly externalizes the shame and alienation it creates in its victims by pointing at the "oppressive" society and blaming normal people and normalcy itself for causing those feelings. The cult becomes the increasingly hermetically sealed social environment for initiates, isolating them more and more from outsiders and outside influences, and the fear of rejection and social isolation keeps people locked into the cult and its cycle of abuse. Many cult members end up emotionally groomed into thinking they cannot live without the cult. For them, the cult is their salvation. Queer Activists threaten a loss of salvation anytime a cult member or initiate steps out of line.

—⁓—

Queer Theory is not merely academic; it is full of religious rituals and observances. The cult distinguishes between in-group and out-group by using "preferred pronouns," complex jargon, and code words in greeting and writing. Queer Activists dress in the religious garb of the drag queen or drag king, or through highly identifiable patterns of dress, grooming, and presentation.

Cultists signal their fealty with a flag that finds itself in constant revolution—a never-ending cascade of additional colors, bars, and symbols stitched into its *queer* fabric. "Agender Pride Day," "International Asexuality Day," "Bisexual Awareness Week," "Genderfluid Visibility Week," "Drag Day," "Intersex Day of Remembrance," "Non-Binary People's Day," "Trans Awareness Month," "Pansexual & Panromantic Awareness Day," and "Pride Month" all mark our calendars with cult celebrations.

Queer Theory demands total submission and obedience. Queer Activists isolate, punish, and exclude anyone who contradicts cult doctrine, ritual, or practice. Family and friends are no exception—if they have a problem with the cult, the cult has a problem with them. The cult psychologically conditions cult members to abandon their loved ones who don't affirm and celebrate an initiate's spiritual awakening. This dynamic guarantees a sense of alienation and isolation together with a belief that only the cult can provide the initiate with friends (or comrades), acceptance, a sense of social identity and belonging, and a "safe" refuge from rejection and loneliness.

Cognitive dissonance is a cult's go-to method for isolating cult members and potential initiates from their friends and families. Cognitive dissonance is the psychological discomfort, stress, and anxiety one feels when one holds two incompatible beliefs. An example of cognitive dissonance is the feeling someone gets when they love animals but eat meat, or when someone supports a political party but disagrees with many of that party's policies. Cognitive dissonance is the crisis you enter when your incompatible beliefs cause emotional turmoil. Should you love animals or eat meat? Should you vote for the party or vote for the policy? Which belief do you betray, and how do you justify the betrayal?

Narcissists are famous for generating cognitive dissonance in those they want to control. They use psychological abuse strategically, introducing a barrage of false information and conflicting beliefs to their targets. Narcissists manipulate their targets, pushing them deep into cognitive dissonance, leaving them confused and unable to trust their perception of reality. The target is easily controlled in this state because they must rely on their abuser to make sense of the world. The cult's inner school becomes the gurus or priests to shepherd the dissonant initiates further into the cult.

The cult of Queer Theory is extremely narcissistic. Cult members are excessively interested in themselves, their appearances, and their religious practices. Queer Activists are control freaks, and they use cognitive dissonance to recruit new members that they want to control. For instance, the cult will tell a girl that, although she looks like a girl, she may be a boy "on the inside" because she plays with certain toys. This generates anxiety and discomfort in the child, who doesn't understand how she can "be a boy" while "looking like a girl." The cult takes advantage of this new vulnerability to brainwash the child. Queer Activists tell her that evil spirits (read: social constructions) control the world, unfairly labeling children "boys" and "girls" and determining everyone's beliefs, attitudes, and behaviors. The cult tells the child that she can reject this unjust and evil influence and begin to free herself from the prison she was born into. The cult tells her she can escape the evil spirits that control how she looks, loves, and acts. Queer Activists coerce the child to take a bite of the apple, introducing to her a special cult knowledge of salvation.

After a child has awakened to this special cult knowledge of salvation, they may naturally want to discuss their excitement with their parents. *Wrong!* Here, the cult sows more cognitive dissonance into the child. Queer Activists tell kids that, although they love their parents, their parents can't understand revelation because they are too old, too stupid, and too brainwashed by the evil spirits that control society. In this sense, their parents are part of the evil spirits' system of control. This system won't accept rule breakers, so the cult tells children their parents won't accept their new cult identity. Queer Activists are known for saying, "If your parents aren't accepting of your identity, I'm your mom now." There's even a hashtag—#freemomhug. You can buy the shirts on Amazon. They are also known for taking pains to redefine the word "family" for initiates as those who accept them for their acceptance of cult doctrine (read: for being "who they really are, authentically") as opposed to the people who would try to protect them from the cult's influences, including flesh and blood family members, especially parents.

Children targeted by the cult love their parents, but they also love the promise of salvation offered to them. The beliefs of their parents, it is suggested, if not outright said, contradict the cult's beliefs. Children learn that evil spirits control their parents. They believe their parents will likely attempt to stop them from attempting their daring escape from the prison that evil spirits have constructed around them. A child must therefore choose between their parents and the cult to resolve their cognitive dissonance. Queer Activists take advantage of this, offering children solutions to manage their crisis, including, but not limited to, adopting a secretive new cult identity at school, changing their name, using the opposite sex's bathrooms, and joining special cult clubs. By doing these things secretly, children aren't upsetting or alerting their parents. At the same time, children get to enjoy their new cult friends and all of the love bombing those friends have in store for them. Queer Activists tell children that Queer Theory is the only way to resolve their anxiety and fear. The cult tells kids that truly loving parents would want them to be happy, even if being happy means keeping secrets.

Of course, the cult has used the same tactics on parents.

Parents are confused when their children suddenly begin fashioning radical new cult identities. In this confusion, parents ask many questions, wanting to know precisely who convinced their children that they were "born in the wrong body." Many parents get furious—rightly so! The cult responds by burying concerned parents in cognitive dissonance and deception. The cult tells parents that the only way to prove that they love their children is to accept, affirm, and celebrate their child's "transition" into their new cult identity. When parents question this approach, Queer Activists launch a barrage of academic-sounding cult words and phrases at them. The cult then tells parents that if they don't affirm their child's new cult identity, they are pushing their child to suicidality. "You love your kid, right?" the cult groomer says. "You'd do anything to protect them, right?" Parents don't want their child to join a cult, but they also don't want their child to commit suicide. The choice is false, but the cult drives it home with deceptive and manipulative techniques that it has spent decades refining. Parents become anxious and scared, and many attempt to resolve their contradictory beliefs by joining the cult themselves. Their old questions, concerns, and fears fold into a *new faith* that the cult knows what is best for their child. Parents begin to think that by handing their child over to the cult, they are loving their child more than ever before. Together, parents and children can fight off evil spirits and free their families from possession.

—–

The cult of Queer Theory has captured our national discussion of sex and sexuality. Queer Activists have waged war on our language and have largely succeeded in convincing the average person that "gender" and "gender identity" are real things. They are not. The terms "gender," as used by the cult, and "gender identity" were invented by the cult.

Astonishingly, Queer Activists have even convinced large swaths of the population that sex isn't real—that "men" and "women" are *political categories.* According to a Pew Research Center study conducted in May of 2022, "Half of adults ages 18 to 29 say someone can be a man or a woman even if that differs from the sex they were assigned at birth. This compares with about four-in-ten of those ages 30 to 49 and about a third of those 50 and older."[1] You will notice that "sex assigned at birth" was used rather than "sex" or "observed sex." The question itself indicates Queer Theory's ascendance in our culture and politics.

Queer Activists have lied, cheated, and bullied their way into all of the places religious cults shouldn't be. Even *Nature,* one of the world's most-read and prestigious scientific journals, publishes cult doctrine.[2] A 2015 article titled "Sex Redefined" argues that *sex isn't binary* and that "Biologists may have been building a more nuanced view of sex, but society has yet to catch up." The article draws its last breath in the final statement, "If you want to know whether someone is male or female, it may be best just to ask."[3] Insanity. Every person can be categorized by whether they possess the reproductive anatomy that, under conditions of normal development, will produce small gametes (sperm) or large gametes (ova) during the period of sexual maturity and fertility. If they can't produce large or small gametes or can produce both (which is exceptionally rare, if it can occur at all), something has gone wrong—there is a defect. There is no third gamete, no

---

1   Pew Research Center. (2022, June 28). *Americans' complex views on gender identity and transgender issues.* Pew Research Center. https://www.pewresearch .org/social-trends/2022/06/28/americans-complex-views-on-gender-identity-and-transgender-issues/

2   Ainsworth, C. (2015). Sex redefined. *Nature,* 518(7539), 288–291.

3   ibid.

intermediate gametes, and no confusion about the fact that bio-logical anomalies sometimes present. More importantly, there is no situation in which a healthy male or female body leaves any ambiguity or confusion about the person's sex. There is no room for nuance. What passes for "nuance" from Queer Activists are distortions and emotional manipulations used as a lever to pry something open so the cult can gain control of it.

It gets worse. The American Psychological Association (APA) not only publishes cult doctrine—it practices cult magic. Regarding doctrine, the APA describes the ascendancy of "gen-der diversity" as "a sea change" that "has hit land and rocked the earth" at "home, in communities, in society, and across the globe."[4] That's one hell of a statement from "the leading scien-tific and professional organization representing psychology in the United States, with more than 146,000 researchers, educators, clinicians, consultants, and students as its members."[5]

As for the practice of cult magic, the APA pushes the "gen-der-affirmative approach," which is the cult's way of forcing both individuals and society to accept Queer Theory. In July of 2023, the APA joined sixty-two other organizations in submitting a letter to Congress that "urg[es] Congress to protect access to gender-af-firming care for transgender youth."[6] The letter, in part, reads:

4   Keo-Meier, C., & Ehrensaft, D. (Eds.). (2018). *The gender affirmative model: An interdisciplinary approach to supporting transgender and gender expansive children.* American Psychological Association.

5   American Psychological Association. (n.d.). *About APA.* American Psychological Association. https://www.apa.org/about/

6   American Psychological Association. (2023, August 9). *Urging Congress to protect access to gender-affirming care for transgender youth.* American Psychological Association. https://www.apaservices.org/advocacy/news/gender-affirming-care-transgender-youth

Health care to treat gender dysphoria is medically necessary, evidence-based care provided to transgender people to alleviate the psychological distress associated with incongruence between an individual's gender and their sex assigned at birth. Gender dysphoria is recognized as a serious medical condition by every major U.S. medical association and the World Health Organization. This health care encompasses mental health counseling, social affirmation (e.g., using a person's chosen name and pronouns), and medical services such as hormone therapy that allow transgender people to live safely and authentically as who they are. Every major medical and mental health association in the U.S., representing more than 1.3 million U.S. doctors, supports individualized, age-appropriate gender-affirming care that promotes the health and well-being of transgender people.[7]

To be clear, these organizations define "transgender" as "anyone whose gender identity differs from their sex assigned at birth."[8] So, the APA, along with sixty-two additional co-conspirators— including the American Psychiatric Association, the American College of Physicians, the Endocrine Society, the National Association of Social Workers, and the Boston Medical Center— have urged Congress to oppose *any* legislation that would prevent the practice of psycho-social, chemical, and surgical intervention on *any* child that "identifies" as anything other than the sex that they are. "Every major medical and mental health association" in the United States is under the cult's spell.

"Gender-affirming care" is cult magic. That's the best way to describe it. Like all cult magic, it plays on the social and emotional

---

7 ibid.
8 Keo-Meier, C., & Ehrensaft, D. (Eds.). (2018). *The gender affirmative model: An interdisciplinary approach to supporting transgender and gender expansive children.* American Psychological Association.

milieu to mystify its targets. As stated, "gender-affirming care" relies on psychological counseling *to affirm the delusional state of the patient* and *social affirmation*, in addition to high-commitment, irreversible interventions like injections of hormones and hormone blockers and surgeries, all tailored to make the cult doctrine come true in the lives and bodies being practiced upon. *Affirmation* is the cult magical process, which is obvious when you realize that standard practice in medicine is to *treat and hopefully cure* pathological states, not *affirm* and further them. Sadly, there are powerful reasons that millions of doctors and mental health professionals now practice the magic—it makes you look "progressive" instead of "bigoted," which is another cult magic spell; there is an enormous demand for it; and there's a ton of money in it.

Queer Activists have been casting spells on administrators, educators, and children for a long time. There is a reason why the people in your life now think that sex, "gender," and sexuality are muddy and confusing. Likewise, there is a reason educators fill your children's classrooms and libraries with pride flags and pornographic books. It would be unimaginable to think that schools would hide a "social transition" from parents in 1980. The terminology to describe such a situation didn't yet exist. There are reasons why all of this is happening, and this book will help you understand those reasons.

What follows will help you understand what the cult of Queer Theory believes, where it comes from, how it got into schools, and what it's attempting to do with children. In *Part One,* we will explain the problem in greater detail. We will also spend a significant amount of time discussing the "theory" of "Queer Theory." It's going to get heavy, and we have all of the confidence in the world that we can make it through some difficult chapters together. Some people want the quick answers—the thirty-thousand-foot summary. We'll cover that, but we'll also cover what Queer Theory is *precisely*. The people who have had only the quick answers have been bulldozed for decades because those people didn't understand what they were dealing with. It's one thing to understand what the cult is doing, and it's another to understand why it is doing what it's doing. If we don't understand the *why*, then we can't understand *how* to reject the magic, protect our children from the cult, and start rebuilding our *normal* lives.

In *Part Two,* we will explore how Queer Theory is practiced in schools. We'll rely heavily on the Queer Theory literature, using Queer Activists' own words to share how they practice Queer Theory on children. We'll touch on how Queer Activists structure their classrooms, how they teach children to practice Queer Theory *on and for* themselves, how they put children into states of crisis that are then "resolved" through Social and Emotional Learning (SEL), and how they "navigate parental resistance" by hiding the whole project from parents.

We wrote *The Queering of the American Child* for anyone who wants to learn about the *queering* of children in our schools. That said, what follows is written with parents and grandparents in mind. I (Logan) am a parent of two young boys. I started researching what's happening in our schools in 2019 because my wife and I were preparing to be parents. I had seen enough in the news to know something was very wrong with our educational system. I've spent the last four years learning everything I can about Queer Theory. For most of this time, I've been nose down in the primary source literature, reading the cult doctrine on its own terms. I've worked countless hours to decipher the cult's coded language. And I do mean "coded"—that's how the cultists describe it. I hope this book can, in many ways, serve as your dictionary so you can decode that language, too.

As we begin *The Queering of the American Child: How Schools Initiate Normal Kids Into the Cult of Queer Theory*, we would like believers and non-believers alike to consider the following question—*What would you do if you thought your children were skipping school to join a religious cult?* It's best to begin thinking about your answers now.

PART 1:
QUEER THEORY

Chapter 1

QUEERING EDUCATION

THE WINSOR SCHOOL

The Winsor School is an elite, all-girls preparatory school in Boston, Massachusetts. At Winsor, parents pay $56,100 a year to prepare their girls to "pursue their aspirations and contribute to the world."[9] For over one hundred years, Winsor has offered exceptional learning opportunities to young women. However, everything changed in 2021 when Winsor pursued a radical agenda, and the girls suddenly disappeared.

It is not normal to see all girls disappear from an all-girls school. But that's precisely what happened at Winsor. In 2021, the school released a 106-page document[10] that outlined a renewed commitment to Diversity, Equity, and Inclusion (DEI). This commitment included a review of Winsor's policies, procedures,

---

9   The Winsor School. (n.d.). *Home.* Retrieved September 6, 2023, from https://www.winsor.edu

10   The Winsor School. (2021). *Lift every voice: A report on diversity, equity, and inclusion at The Winsor School.* https://bbk12e1-cdn.myschoolcdn.com/ftpimages/1082/misc/misc_206046.pdf

practices, and professional development training. The goal was to "seek a deeper understanding of the totality of our DEI practices" and to "provide a roadmap to the work ahead."[11] A central feature of that roadmap was eliminating the use of *gendered language* at the school.

The Winsor School's commitment to DEI meant that the adults in the room were no longer committed to protecting and educating girls. In practice, the commitment erased girls altogether. In *Lift Every Voice: A Report on Diversity, Equity, and Inclusion At The Winsor School*, Winsor's administration makes this point clear:

> Winsor has...adopted changes to its use of gendered language and pronouns to be more inclusive. External publications and communications have moved away from using "she, her, hers" and "your daughter," replacing the former with "they, them, theirs" and the latter with "student." Sensitivity is also paid to family structure. In Admission, for example, interviews are now called the "Adult family member interview" instead of the "Parent/guardian interview." Faculty and staff are discouraged from addressing groups of students as "girls" and "ladies," and teachers address students by their preferred pronouns.[12]

How does a commitment to something like "inclusion" lead to the radical proposition that it is no longer OK to call girls "girls" *at an all-girls' school*? Why does embracing "inclusion" mean it is wrong to call parents "parents"? It's not normal for an all-girls school to stop calling groups of young women "ladies." So, why did Winsor do this?

The *Lift Every Voice* report answers these questions indirectly.

---

11   ibid.
12   ibid.

Throughout the document, The Winsor School's administration suggests that The Winsor School is an institution that, despite its best efforts, treats some students unfairly. For this reason, Winsor's teachers "are expected to…build an inclusive curriculum; respond to individual and institutional prejudices, both overt and subtle; and actively seek to dismantle systems of oppression."[13] To that end, The Winsor School "funds professional development for the necessary training and skill development related to these expectations." *DEI-focused professional development opportunities for faculty and staff 2018–present*, found in *Appendix D* of *Lift Every Voice*, lists several of these trainings—*Answering the Call of Social Justice; Implicit Bias: Peanut Butter, Jelly, and Racism; Gender and Sexual Diversity: An Exploration*, to name a few.

In 2010, Forbes named Winsor one of America's top-ten prep schools. According to the Census Bureau, the per capita income in Massachusetts is less than Winsor's yearly tuition. The girls attending Winsor are some of the most privileged in the country, so how do we make sense of this document? Likewise, how do we make sense of the following statement from Winsor's Director of Admission and Financial Aid?

> Winsor started doing [DEI work] long before other schools. Yet there are people still having experiences here that leave them feeling like an outsider, or like they're not a full member of the Winsor community. That is what we need to be critical of in our own practice, in our institution. How do we disrupt that?[14]

GENDER BUREAUCRACY

To better understand what happened at Winsor, we will look

---

13   ibid.
14   ibid.

at another institution that introduced a confusing document in 2021—the U.S. Department of Education (USDE). The document, *Supporting Transgender Youth In Schools*, states that "As the Department of Education has reaffirmed, discrimination based on sex—including sexual orientation and gender identity—isn't just wrong, it's prohibited in America's schools."[15] Including the term "gender identity" in a statement about *sexual* discrimination doesn't make any sense. According to the American Psychological Association (APA), "gender identity" is defined as "an internal sense of being male, female, or something else, which may or may not correspond to an individual's sex assigned at birth or sex characteristics."[16] What does an *internal sense* of one's sex or "gender" have anything to do with the reality of one's sex? There are only two sexes, male and female, and a person's sex is *observed* at birth, not assigned. How can sexual discrimination be reinterpreted to include discrimination against *feelings* rather than an essential characteristic? Whatever the reasoning, the message was clear—the USDE considers "gender identity" a protected category. A student's feelings about "what they are on the inside" can no longer be questioned in America's schools.

Supporting Transgender Youth In Schools lists many new policies and practices that schools can consider developing to "ensure that all students…are safe and supported." The first recommendation is that schools use "welcoming and inclusive" language and commit to "ensuring a safe and supportive campus that is free from discrimination and harassment for LGBTQ+ students." This was clearly reflected in the Winsor documentation as well. The USDE also recommends that school policies "clearly

15   U.S. Department of Education. (2021, June). *Supporting transgender youth in school*. U.S. Department of Education, Office for Civil Rights. https://www2.ed.gov/about/offices/list/ocr/docs/ed-factsheet-transgender-202106.pdf
16   American Psychological Association. (2018, September 1). *Defining transgender terms*. Monitor on Psychology, 49(8).

affirm students' right to be free from discrimination based on sexual orientation or gender identity." This also helps us make sense of the statement from Winsor's Director of Admission and Financial Aid about students feeling like "full members of the Winsor community."

Shockingly, the U.S. Department of Education also recommends that schools adopt policies that "respect" students by allowing kids to use different names and pronouns while in school. *Supporting Transgender Youth In Schools* goes as far as saying that schools should think about adopting "model plans" to "guide school staff on how to support students...in any *transition* [emphasis added] process."

This isn't just a U.S. Department of Education initiative. Though it goes too far beyond the intention of this chapter or book to go into the details—which would deserve several detailed chapters, at the least—much of the sex, "gender," sexuality, and sexual education in schools all over the world today is there because of a broad program called *Comprehensive Sexuality Education (CSE)*. CSE was originally developed in the early 2000s at the United Nations Educational, Scientific, and Cultural Organization (UNESCO), and is pushed to all member states from there as a part of "inclusive" and "global citizenship" education. It is directly tied to using education to help achieve the United Nations Agenda 2030 "Sustainable Development Goals" (SDGs), including Goals 4 ("quality education for all") and 5 ("gender equality") especially, but also Goals 3 ("good health and well-being"), 8 ("decent work and economic growth"), and 10 ("reduce inequalities"), if not others. Reaching far beyond traditional sex education, which is predominantly medical and anatomical and focused on risk-, pregnancy-, and disease-prevention, Comprehensive Sexuality Education includes as core curriculum topics on sex, "gender," and sexuality, all deeply informed by Queer Theory. Alarmingly, it also includes as two of its seven "pillars" lessons on "sexual citizenship" and "pleasure-based sexual education," the first of which is informed throughout by Critical Theory and the second by Queer Theory. Though the sex education standards in the United States are decided at the state level in each state, CSE has been fully adopted by several states, including California and Oregon, and an influential campaign coordinated by organizations like SIECUS (Sexuality Information and Education Council of the United States) and Planned Parenthood pushes to continue its expansion, even down to the Pre–K level. Comprehensive Sexuality Education is also endorsed by a dazzling array of professional organizations discussed elsewhere in this book, including the American Medical Association (AMA), American Psychological Association (APA), and the American Academy of Pediatrics (AAP).

To summarize, the highest educational institution in the land, ostensibly following the guidance of some of the largest international, activist, and professional organizations in the world, pushes schools to accept "the fact" that each of their students has a "gender identity." The U.S. Department of Education is also pushing schools to create administrative policies and practices to affirm the gender identities of their students. These affirmative practices don't have any limiting principles. If a child feels like they are "something else," the schools are encouraged to treat those feelings as a matter-of-fact. Ultimately, these mechanisms of milieu control will expand until they are recognized for what they are and are stopped.

Whereas the *Supporting Transgender Youth In Schools* document makes many recommendations, the U.S. Department of Education's Office For Civil Rights (OCR) makes a lot of requirements:

The mission of the U.S. Department of Education's Office for Civil Rights (OCR) is to ensure equal access to education and to promote educational excellence through vigorous enforcement of civil rights in our nation's schools. To serve this mission, OCR enforces civil rights laws to protect all students from unlawful discrimination and harassment based on race, color, national origin, sex, disability, and age. This includes students who are lesbian, gay, bisexual, transgender, queer, questioning, asexual, intersex, nonbinary, or identify their sexual orientation or gender identity in other ways (LGBTQI+).[17]

According to the OCR, schools that refuse to affirm a student's "gender identity" directly violate civil rights laws. From the OCR's perspective, schools are now required by law to restructure their curriculum, practices, policies, and procedures to affirm student feelings. I don't remember the Civil Rights Act of 1964 including "gender identity" as a protected category. How has the OCR reached this conclusion?

In June 2020, the United States Supreme Court ruled on *Bostock v. Clayton County, Georgia*. Gerald Bostock, a gay man working for Clayton County as a child welfare services coordinator, was fired for "conduct unbecoming of its employees." Bostock filed a lawsuit against the county, alleging discrimination based on sexual orientation. Bostock's case reached the U.S. Supreme Court, where it was consolidated with two other cases, *Altitude Express Inc. v. Zarda* and *R.G. & G.R. Harris Funeral Homes Inc. v. EEOC*. The question before the Court was this: Does Title VII of the Civil Rights Act of 1964, which prohibits employment discrimination "because of...sex" encompass discrimination based on a person's sexual orientation or transgender status?

---

17   U.S. Department of Education. (n.d.). *About OCR*. Retrieved from https://www2.ed.gov/about/offices/list/ocr/aboutocr.html

Justice Gorsuch delivered the opinion of the Court, which stated that "an employer who fires an individual merely for being gay or transgender violates Title VII." Including a person's "transgender" status is key here because a person who is transgender is *identifying* with a sex other than *their sex*. In his majority opinion, Gorsuch wrote:

> Or take an employer who fires a transgender person who was identified as a male at birth but who now identifies as a female. If the employer retains an otherwise identical employee who was identified as female at birth, the employer intentionally penalizes a person identified as male at birth for traits or actions that it tolerates in an employee identified as female at birth. Again, the individual employee's sex plays an unmistakable and impermissible role in the discharge decision.[18]

The Court's decision, therefore, interprets Title VII to prohibit employment discrimination based on sex, sexual orientation, *and* transgender status, which is but one of many possible "gender identities" one can claim. So, the Court now interprets Title VII to include "gender identity," which is not an essential characteristic of one's person, as a protected category.

The logic of the Court's majority opinion is seductive but flawed. This is a crucial point that requires a reply. The heart of the question is this: "If an employer takes an employment action solely because of the sexual orientation or gender identity of an employee or applicant, has that employer necessarily discriminated because of...sex?" As the dissenting opinion by Justice Alito makes clear, the answer should be "No." Neither a person's

---

18 Supreme Court of the United States. (2019). *Bostock v. Clayton County, Georgia*. Retrieved from https://www.supremecourt.gov/opinions/19pdf/17-1618_hfci.pdf

sexual orientation nor "gender identity" is tied to either of the sexes. That is, both males and females can be sexually attracted to people of their own sex and identify as different "genders." An employer would not be discriminating on the basis of sex if they implemented a blanket policy against hiring homosexuals and "trans" identifying individuals without knowing the sex of the job applicants. What is being discriminated against is the behavior of choosing to identify contrary to the facts of one's sex, which some members of both sexes do. The attorney representing the employees in the case said so herself, admitting the "fatal" flaw in the Court's interpretation. As Alito explains:

> The attorney's concession was necessary, but it is fatal to the Court's interpretation, for if an employer discriminates against individual applicants or employees without even knowing whether they are male or female, it is impossible to argue that the employer intentionally discriminated because of sex…An employer cannot intentionally discriminate on the basis of a characteristic of which the employer has no knowledge. And if an employer does not violate Title VII by discriminating on the basis of sexual orientation or gender identity without knowing the sex of the affected individuals, there is no reason why the same employer could not lawfully implement the same policy even if it knows the sex of these individuals. If an employer takes an adverse employment action for a perfectly legitimate reason—for example, because an employee stole company property—that action is not converted into sex discrimination simply because the employer knows the employee's sex. As explained, a disparate treatment case requires proof of intent—i.e., that the employee's sex motivated the firing. In short, what this example shows is that discrimination because of sexual orientation or gender identity does not inherently or necessarily

entail discrimination because of sex, and for that reason, the Court's chief argument collapses.

That isn't the interpretation that ruled the day, however, and the consequences can and will expand. On June 22nd, 2021, following the Court's decision in *Bostock v. Clayton County*, the U.S. Department of Education's OCR issued a notice of interpretation regarding Title IX. As originally interpreted, Title IX protects persons from *sexual* discrimination. However, the OCR's notice of interpretation stated that the OCR "will fully enforce Title IX to prohibit discrimination based on sexual orientation and gender identity in education programs and activities that receive Federal financial assistance from the Department."[19] Furthermore:

> This includes allegations of individuals being harassed, disciplined in a discriminatory manner, excluded from, denied equal access to, or subjected to sex stereotyping in academic or extracurricular opportunities and other education programs or activities, denied the benefits of such programs or activities, or otherwise treated differently because of their sexual orientation or gender identity.[20]

All public and private elementary and secondary schools, school districts, colleges, and universities receiving *any* federal financial assistance must comply with Title IX. Title IX states, "No person in the United States shall, on the basis of sex, be excluded from participation in, be denied the benefits of, or be subjected to discrimination under any education program or activity receiving

---

19 U.S. Department of Education. (2021, June). *Notice of interpretation: Enforcement of Title IX of the Education Amendments of 1972 with respect to discrimination based on sexual orientation and gender identity in light of Bostock v. Clayton County*. U.S. Department of Education, Office for Civil Rights. https://www2.ed.gov/about/offices/list/ocr/docs/202106-titleix-noi.pdf
20 ibid.

Federal financial assistance." You will notice that gender identity is not mentioned. The U.S. Department of Education's OCR doesn't care, and it now has a significant ruling to hide behind.

Interpreting Title IX in light of Title VII has devastating consequences for education, but it does allow us to see the truly fatal flaw in Justice Gorsuch's reasoning for the Court. The most obvious of these consequences is related to the language of "exclusion" and "access." To make these consequences clear, consider this: If a male identifying as a female enters a female-only space—a bathroom or changing room, for example—and is removed from that space for not being female, then the basis of his exclusion is his sex. Using Gorsuch's reasoning, a female identifying as a female to enter the space would not be excluded while a male identifying as a female would. But such a space is sex-segregated and is reserved for females only, so the male's exclusion is justified by definition. If both males and females can enter a sex-segregated female-only space, then that space is no longer sex-segregated, which is a *functional contradiction*. If it is no longer sex-segregated, then sex doesn't matter, and one can't claim sex discrimination as the basis of their exclusion. You can't say a space is sex-segregated for females only but simultaneously allow in a male who *identifies* as female because in that moment you admit that sex is a hollow category that cannot be the basis for segregating spaces. In this example, sex can't be claimed as the basis for discrimination in any way whatsoever. Sex-segregated spaces demand that sex is substantive and essential, so a male cannot meaningfully identify as a female and enter a female-only space. You can't have it both ways. A space is either sex-segregated or it is not. Trying to split the middle this way evacuates the category of sex of its essential meaning, and that in turn would prevent applying Title IX or Title VII because its basis, sex, is now empty.

An individual's sex either means "sex" in education or it doesn't. The Court and the OCR side with "it doesn't." Eliminating the distinction means that an individual can identify as whatever sex they would like, using that constitutionally protected *political position* as grounds for trampling a constitutionally protected class (sex) of another party.

THE SPECTER

The Department of Education's recent statements regarding Title IX aren't all that surprising. The OCR started interpreting Title IX through a radical lens years ago. The OCR simply feels more confident in its determination now.

In 2014, the OCR released *Questions and Answers on Title IX and Sexual Violence*, following the 2011 *Dear Colleague Letter* "on student-on-student sexual harassment and sexual violence." In *Questions and Answers*, the OCR stated that Title IX:

> prohibits gender-based harassment, which may include acts of verbal, nonverbal, or physical aggression, intimidation, or hostility based on sex or sex-stereotyping. Thus, it can be sex discrimination if students are harassed either for exhibiting what is perceived as a stereotypical characteristic for their sex, or for failing to conform to stereotypical notions of masculinity and femininity. Title IX also prohibits sexual harassment and gender-based harassment of all students, regardless of the actual or perceived sexual orientation or gender identity of the harasser or target.[21]

The U.S. Department of Education's OCR, thus all schools

21   U.S. Department of Education. (2014, April 29). *Questions and answers on Title IX and sexual violence* [Archived version]. U.S. Department of Education, Office for Civil Rights. https://web.archive.org/web/20140429210445/http://www2.ed.gov/about/offices/list/ocr/docs/qa-201404-title-ix.pdf

receiving federal dollars, has interpreted Title IX in light of "gender identity" for over a decade. During that time, school district administrators and educators rushed to develop new curriculum, policies, practices, and procedures to "affirm" and celebrate their students' gender identities. As they did so, a new cult religion, both the catalyst of the recent radical demands to restructure schools *and* the wholesale provider of solutions to meet them, rushed through the front door.

Queer Theory, an activist discipline in the strictest possible sense—the activists are disciplined, and the discipline is activism—has completely captured school districts nationwide. Where did the U.S. Department of Education's OCR get the idea that "gender identity" is a real thing and that all children have one? Where did it get the idea that children are discriminated against based on their gender identity? Why is the OCR acting more like an activist organization, pushing schools to adopt interpretations of law that are functionally contradictory? Why does the U.S. Department of Education suggest that children can "transition" from one sex or gender to another?

Queer Theory is the answer to these questions. Queer Theory openly embraces not only transition but also that functional contradiction because contradictions are useful for creating the type of confusion that advances their activism. That is, Queer Theory views contradictions as *queer*. Only awakened Queer Activists can resolve the contradictions correctly, so embracing contradictions gives them power.

Of course, what we have seen in the above is the cult of Queer Theory being applied to The Winsor School, through the U.S. Department of Education, and through its OCR. The cult magic that looks to use specialist language and milieu control to negate physical reality is on full display. "Gendered language" has to be eliminated to create a context in which cult doctrine can override physical reality, and a political and social environment is being established in which the magic "works."

While typically not mentioned by name, Queer Theory is the foundation on which the U.S. Department of Education's *Supporting Transgender Youth In Schools* document rests. In fact, Queer Theory is the foundation of most—if not all—school policies related to sex, gender, and sexuality in America today. There are telltale signs we can look for to confirm the presence of Queer Theory in schools, all of which litter the USDE's official website and releases. Any mention of the following terms and phrases in school policies, procedures, or curriculum indicate Queer Theory's contamination: "gender identity," "cisgender," "non-binary," "gender expression," "sex assigned at birth," "transgender," "intersectional," "LGBTQ+," "social/legal/medical transition."

There are additional signs that are harder to spot for the untrained eye. Queer Theory is found in all Diversity, Equity, and Inclusion (DEI) statements, commitments, and frameworks. Everywhere you find DEI, you find Queer Theory. This is because the theory DEI is rooted in is "intersectional" and includes critical (read: Woke) analysis of race, sex, gender, sexuality, and all the rest woven together so that it isn't permissible to consider some of them without considering all of them. Queer Theory is the dominant mode of analysis for sex, gender, and sexuality among these.

Sometimes a DEI statement will mention Queer Theory explicitly. At other times, you can find it lurking in citations. However, most of the time you must dig deeper, removing layers of deception to reveal Queer Theory's undeniable presence. In these instances, Queer Theory only appears absent, but you can find it buried in the justifications for needing DEI practices and in the solutions DEI provides to meet those demands.

For instance, you find Queer Theory in the argument that

schools need to be "safe" and "inclusive." You don't find Queer Theory named explicitly in *Lifting Every Voice*. However, you do find the word "safe" mentioned sixteen times, "inclusive" mentioned thirty-nine times, and "inclusion" mentioned a walloping forty-nine times! If you're unfamiliar with Queer Theory, seeing the words "safe," "inclusive," and "inclusion" mentioned on every other line is cause for confusion. It only makes sense for a school administration to fixate and obsess over these words if they think they are waging a war against "exclusion." As *Lift Every Voice* makes clear, this is precisely what The Winsor School administration thinks. The school moved away from using gendered language because "assuming a person's gender" is an *exclusionary act*. If you assume that all girls in your all-girls classroom are girls, you exclude the girls who *identify* differently. Likewise, you exclude LGBTQ+ "identities" if you don't "ensure that underrepresented voices and experiences share significant weight in the curriculum." In short, if you don't practice Queer Theory, you're not doing "inclusion" correctly, and you can't make your space a "safe" one for people with radicalized "identities."

So, what is Queer Theory? Queer Theory is a theory of how society works. Specifically, it's a theory of how society determines what our standards, rules, and norms are, especially as those standards, rules, and norms relate to sex, gender, and sexuality. Queer Theory assumes that all norms are "regulated and connected to social power."[22] Queer Theory sets out to examine and critique how this social power manifests itself in the way we communicate, draw distinctions between things, and build categories.

---

22 McCann, H., & Monaghan, W. (Eds.). (2017). *Queer Theory Now*. Cambridge Scholars Publishing

> Queer Theory goes beyond exploring aspects of gay and lesbian
> identity and experience. It questions take-for-granted assumptions
> about relationships, identity, gender, and sexual orientation. It seeks
> to explode rigid normalizing categories.[23] (Meyer, 2007, p. 15)

Queer Theory is also a practice, meaning it's not just a way to
think about the world—it's also something you *do* to change
it. This can be confusing because we don't typically associate a
theory with action. The theory of gravity, for example, doesn't tell
us what we *ought to do*. The theory of gravity only describes what
our current understanding of gravity is. Likewise, we don't find
values buried in the theory of electromagnetism or cell theory.
Queer Theory is altogether different—the theory and practice of
Queer Theory are inseparable. Queer Theory is both a theory and
a practice, often described as "praxis."

A basketball team reviews their playbook before game time.
The team has a theory of how they can score more points than the
opposing team. A player on this team competes at center court
for a jump ball that starts the game, setting the team's theory of
how they can win into practice. Queer Theory works similarly.
Queer Activists—those who believe that Queer Theory is a fac-
tual description of how society works—take their theory into the
world and agitate for social change through political activism.
The basketball team's goal is to score more points. The Queer
Activist's goal is to change society.

> Queer activists often work to expose problems in the status quo
> and help us imagine and create more socially just alternatives.
> They work to change laws and policies by lobbying legislators or
> staging protests, they teach others to break through glass ceilings

---

23   Meyer, E. J. (2007). *But I'm not Gay: What Straight Teachers Need to Know
about Queer Theory*. Peter Lang Publishing.

or challenge discriminatory employment or housing or healthcare practices, they organize community or school groups for political action.[24] (Kumashiro, 2009, p. 53)

The practice of Queer Theory is called "queering." The word "queer," in this sense, is a verb. "To queer" is "to destabilize the social, cultural, and political normalizing structures that work to solidify identities and in doing so skew power toward the "norm."[25] Put simply, "to queer" is to challenge and eliminate *normalcy*. "Normalcy" means "the condition of being normal, as in usual, typical, or expected." So, *to queer* is to challenge and eliminate the idea that anything can or should be considered normal.

In brief, Queer Theory adopts the disposition that certain people illegitimately declared themselves to be "normal" and branded everyone else "abnormal," "deviant," even "degenerate" and "perverse" in order to include themselves in mainstream society and marginalize the *Others*. This designation of "normal" is therefore not grounded in facts about the realities of being human, including our patterns of social interaction, nor is it merely arbitrary; it is explicitly self-serving and political thus *unjust* and in need of *disruption and dismantling*. Its goal, therefore, could be summarized in a single sentence: abolish what people agree to call "normalcy."

Queer Theory "is at heart about politics."[26] Queer Theory's fundamental argument is that all norms carry political agendas.

---

24   Kumashiro, K. K. (2009). *Against common sense: Teaching and learning toward social justice*. Routledge.
25   Burnes, T. R., Stanley, J. L., & Miville, M. L. (Eds.). (2017). *Teaching LGBTQ psychology: Queering innovative pedagogy and practice*. American Psychological Association
26   Wilchins, R. (2004). *Queer Theory, gender theory: An instant primer*. Alyson Publications. (p. 5).

Queer Activists believe these political agendas are hidden in "common sense" attitudes, beliefs, and behaviors.

> what society defines as common sense may appear to be just the way things are, but they actually are social constructs that function to "confirm and reinforce...structurally generated relations of domination." What society defines as common sense justifies the oppressive status quo of society by sustaining "the appearance of the world as given and received, and of reality as existing on its own." Commonsense discourses, then, not only socialize us to accept oppressive conditions as "normal" and the way things are, but also to make these conditions normative and the way things ought to be.[27] (Kumashiro, 2002, p. 82)

Queer Activists believe that the only reason people believe anything is normal or natural is because those people have been brainwashed to believe so through a half-organic process called "socialization." For what it's worth, the Marxist phrasing for the "half-organic process" of socialization would be saying something like "normalcy is a historical process" which Queer Theory seeks to identify and transform to its own purposes. In this view, powerful people and institutions use the cover of science, objectivity, reason, and rationality to mask an unfair social hierarchy that grants privilege to those people considered "normal" while marginalizing those considered abnormal or deviant. It is for this reason that Queer Theory seeks to abolish all norms.

Queer Activists *queer* norms, institutions, and society because they believe they must do so to eliminate oppression.

---

27 Kumashiro, K. K. (2002). Against repetition: Addressing resistance to anti-oppressive change in the practices of learning, teaching, supervising, and researching. *Harvard Educational Review, 72*(1), 67–93.

Queer Activists think they must practice their political activism until society no longer considers *anything* normal—until we all live, as Queer Activist Michael Warner describes it, on a *queer planet*.[28]

QUEER EDUCATION

Queer Theory operates like a virus—indeed, while this is meant as criticism of its behavior, it is also how scholars have described it themselves, calling it an "ideal metaphor" for their behavior.[29] It first incubated in Women's Studies and Lesbian and Gay Studies throughout the 1980s. The virus reached full maturity in the 1990s after the likes of Gayle Rubin, Judith Butler, Eve Kosofsky Sedgwick, Teresa de Lauretis, Michael Warner, and David Halperin performed their gain-of-function research, creating a wholly distinct academic field—Queer Studies.

Queer Theory spread rapidly out of the purple-hair departments in what Queer Theorist Riki Wilchins calls an "amazing conquest of academia,"[30] finding a home in every place it didn't belong. Every discipline has standards, rules, traditions, and norms—receptor sites—that Queer Theory latched onto. Queer Activists marched out of their incubators throughout the 1990s and through the front door of philosophy, sociology, communication studies, history, and political science lecture halls. Queer Activists demanded a say in these disciplines, arguing that no one understood how unjust and oppressive their fields were, and took "no" as proof of exactly the bigotry they said no one could

---

28   Warner, M. (1991). Introduction: Fear of a queer planet. *Social Text*, (29), 3–17.

29   Fahs, B., & Karger, M. (2016). Women's studies as virus: Institutional feminism, affect, and the projection of danger. *GÉNEROS. Multidisciplinary Journal of Gender Studies*, 5(1), 929–957.

30   Wilchins, R. (2004). *Queer Theory, gender theory: An instant primer*. Alyson Publications. (p. 21).

understand without them and their unique perspective. Queer Activists claimed "the truth" of how society works and used academic activism to make Queer Theory interdisciplinary. In short, Queer Activists *queered* the university system by changing how everyone in that system thought about traditions, standards, rules, norms, and knowledge itself.

The field of education was no exception. Queer Theory weaseled its way into education immediately, and by 1993 Mary Bryson and Suzanne de Castell had published their landmark paper *Queer Pedagogy: Praxis Makes Im/Perfect.* In the paper, Bryson and de Castell "wanted to make Queer Theory explicitly activist in nature"[31] and argued for a "queer pedagogy," which they defined as "a radical form of educative praxis implemented deliberately to interfere with, to intervene in, the production of 'normalcy' in schooled subjects."

> It seems that a worthwhile avenue for the elucidation of a queer praxis might be to consider the value of an actively queerying pedagogy — of queering its technics and scribbling graffiti over its texts, of colouring outside of the lines so as to deliberately take the wrong route on the way to school — going in an altogether different direction than that specified by a monologic destination. This seems a promising approach indeed for refashioning pedagogy.[32] (Bryson & de Castell, 1993, p. 299)

Bryson and Castell called on educators to apply Queer Theory—both the theory of how society works and the strategies to change it—in their classrooms. Said another way, the authors suggested

---

31   Seal, M. (2019). *The interruption of heteronormativity in higher education: Critical queer pedagogies.* Springer. (p. 60).

32   Bryson, M., & de Castell, S. (1993). Queer pedagogy: Praxis makes im/perfect. *Canadian Journal of Education / Revue canadienne de l'éducation*, 18(3), 285–305.

that Queer Activists work to *queer* schools. Bryson and Castell called on Queer Activists to "deliberately…interfere with" the production of *normal kids*. Children who learn how to be normal in school, so the argument goes, serve to reproduce the norms of society. Queer Theory's central goal is to eliminate norms, and Queer Activists knew then, as they do now, that they must first break the *normal child* if they want to break the *normal society*.

Other Queer Activists quickly followed in the footsteps of Bryson and Castell. Deborah P. Britzmann published *Is there a queer pedagogy? Or, stop reading straight* in 1995, and Susanne Luhmann published *Queering/Querying Pedagogy? Or, Pedagogy Is a Pretty Queer Thing* in 1998. By 1999, James T. Sears had published *Queering Elementary Education: Advancing the dialogue about sexualities and schooling*. A Queer Theory of Education was off to the races, zooming through classrooms and computer screens, and no standards or rules would stop it.

Queer Activists have been queering schools for the last thirty years. Today, administrators, curriculum developers, and teachers look to papers like *Queering Elementary Education: A Queer Curriculum For 4th Grade* to inform how they can make their schools and classrooms more "inclusive."

During Unit 2, 4th graders begin to make their own personal dictionaries to keep track of the terminology they will be learning such as cisgender, transgender, non-binary, and agender. Key learning goals include understanding the differences between assigned sex and gender identity, identifying various pronouns, and analyzing the gender binary. Students begin independently reading George by Alex Gino, a middle grade novel about a trans girl, and they discuss the text in small groups. Using children's picture books to aid them, the students brainstorm stereotypes associated with gender, race, and other identity categories and discuss how these can affect individuals.[33] (Butensky & Brown, 2021, p. 60)

As we have been phrasing it, in other words, Queer Activists sought to install the terminology of the cult of Queer Theory in schools as early as possible. When children are educated to believe these terms are commonly used and understood, they will locate meaning in them and define themselves and the world on their terms. In that way, the innocence of children is taken advantage of in a very subtle way to normalize and spread the cult doctrine while quietly initiating generations.

The fact is, Queer Activists have waged war on the categories of sex, "gender," and sexuality for decades. These radicals have taken their war into our schools, which are now saturated with Queer Theory. So ubiquitous is Queer Theory that it is now synonymous with "inclusive" policies, procedures, and learning.

School children now learn that every person has a "gender identity" that may or may not match their sex. In other words, children are learning that a thing called "gender identity" exists and that it is wholly untethered from a person's biology. Children learn that just because you are born a male doesn't mean you are a male, and just because you are born a female doesn't mean you are a female. A person can "become" a male or a female, regardless of their sex.

In schools nationwide, in both "red" and "blue" states, educators tell children that an ideology called "cisheteronormativity" permeates all aspects of society. Cisheteronormativity refers to the assumption or belief that being "cisgender" (identifying with your "sex assigned at birth") and heterosexual (being attracted

---

33 Butensky, E., & Brown, K. W. (2021). Queering elementary education: A queer curriculum for 4th grade. *Journal of Critical Education Policy Studies at Swarthmore College*, 3(1), Article 4.

to the opposite sex) *has been made* the norm or standard in society. In other words, children are learning that it's not normal to "identify" with your "sex assigned at birth," and it's not normal to be heterosexual. Children learn that the only reason society considers those things normal is because people with power and privilege have made it so for reasons that are explicitly self-serving and unjust.

Queer Theory isn't presented to children as the gigantic academic cult discipline it is. Queer Theory is distilled down for easy, colorful, and fun consumption, taking shape through cute-looking cartoons in the "genderbread person" and the "gender unicorn." Through children's books, posters, Comprehensive Sexuality Education (CSE—a project formulated at and promoted by UNESCO, the United Nations Educational, Scientific, and Cultural Organization, to all its member states), and Social and Emotional Learning (SEL) exercises, kids learn that their "gender identity" is "how you think about yourself." They also learn that their "gender expression" is "how you demonstrate your gender through the ways you act, dress, behave, and interact." Make no mistake, these are cult doctrines.

Queer Activists have transformed educational policies, practices, and content to align with, forward, and put into practice their radical cult religion. They have repurposed education to *queer* the healthy minds and bodies of *normal* kids. In fact, they have gone so far as to insist that there are no truly normal kids because there is no such thing as true normal and thus that all kids—therefore all people—are intrinsically queer and waiting to find it out. For example, queer education activist Lindz Amer posted to Twitter on June 14, 2022,

When I talk about queer, trans, & non-binary kids, I'm not just talking about kids who *currently* identify as such. I'm talking about ALL KIDS. Bc all kids are queer. Queer as in different, non-normative, & pre-structural. That's why kids are vital to liberation movements [sic][34]

Queer Educators are not concerned with teaching kids to read, write, do mathematics, or become normal adults. Queer Educators are only concerned with radicalizing children—*all* children. Queer Theory teaches kids to denounce our current society—all standards, rules, definitions, categories, and traditions—at every conceivable level while simultaneously announcing new *queer possibilities*. As stated by José Esteban Muñoz in his 2009 book *Cruising Utopia,*

> Queerness is not yet here. Queerness is an ideality. Put another way, we are not yet queer. We may never touch queerness, but we can feel it as the warm illumination of a horizon imbued with potentiality. We have never been queer, yet queerness exists for us as an ideality that can be distilled from the past and used to imagine a future. The future is queerness's domain. Queerness is a structuring and educated mode of desiring that allows us to see and feel beyond the quagmire of the present. The here and now is a prison house.[35]
> (Muñoz, 2009, p. 1)

Disturbingly, Queer Activists are obsessed with schools. They know that if they can control the schools, they can brainwash future generations to root out and eliminate all normalcy in society. Their deconstructive campaign has been so successful that school administrators and teachers nationwide now believe

---

34   Amer, L. [@lindzamer]. (2022, June 14). When I talk about queer, trans, & non-binary kids, I'm not just talking about kids who currently identify as such. I'm talking about ALL KIDS. Bc all kids are queer. Queer as in different, non-normative, & pre-structural. That's why kids are vital to liberation movements [Tweet]. Twitter

35   Muñoz J. E. (2009). *Cruising Utopia: The then and there of queer futurity.* New York University Press.

that children can be "born in the wrong body"; so successful that teachers legitimately believe that they can't tell what a student's sex is by looking at them; so successful that an all-girls school no longer thinks it's OK to call girls "girls."

What does a queer school look like? It looks like your typical K–12 school today. Queer schools have firmly entrenched DEI commitments, policies, and practices. They have new language codes and rules designed to suppress dissent and enforce ideological conformity. Queer schools are less focused on learning traditional subjects and more focused on an endless barrage of psycho-social and emotional manipulations. They are full of pride flags, pornographic books, drag queens, and religious cult rituals.

Queer Activists have transformed education's purpose, methods, and content to push kids to become Queer Activists themselves. They have determined that the best way to do this is to teach kids to *queer themselves*—to teach kids to destabilize their minds and bodies by deconstructing their identity until they become *queer*, which is a *political cult identity* that has nothing to do with sex, "gender," or sexuality. In the words of world-renowned Queer Theorist David Halperin, *queer* is "an identity without an essence."[36] *Whoa*. In full context, he gives away the game: "queer" is a wholly political stance against normalcy and legitimacy and has little or nothing to do with homosexuality itself. He writes,

> Unlike gay identity, which, though deliberately proclaimed in an act of affirmation, is nonetheless rooted in the positive fact of homosexual object-choice, queer identity need not be grounded in any positive truth or in any stable reality. As the very word implies, "queer" does not name some natural kind or refer to some

---

36   Halperin, D. M. (1995). *Saint Foucault: Towards a gay hagiography*. Oxford University Press. (p. 61).

determinate object; it acquires its meaning from its oppositional relation to the norm. Queer is by definition *whatever* is at odds with the normal, the legitimate, the dominant. *There is nothing in particular to which it necessarily refers.* It is an identity without an essence. (Halperin, 1995, p. 62, italics in original)

Queer Activism is dedicated to disrupting normalcy wherever it manifests, by definition. That means it is also dedicated to preventing any sense of normalcy from ever taking root in children in the first place. Queer Activists say that the idea of a healthy and innocent child, both in mind and body, is a political construction created to maintain a "developmental sequence which culminates in normalcy."[37] Said another way, Queer Activists think there is no such thing as a "healthy and innocent" child. They think those in power created and defined the categories of "healthy" and "innocent" to coerce society to raise children a certain way. In this sense, all children are compared to "normal" and "healthy" childhood development to sort out those children that will help reproduce society as it is, cementing the *normal* status quo. Queer Activists don't recognize boundaries, so they think all children are fair game. A *queer education* first reduces vulnerable children to empty vessels and then fills them with revolutionary political programming.

If Queer Activists reduce children to empty categories, then there is no longer anything society can point to and say, "We must protect *that*." Queer Activists have, in many cases, successfully blurred the boundaries between adult and child, with the ultimate goal of collapsing those boundaries altogether. Queer Activists will tell you, as Minnesota Lt. Governor Peggy Flanagan did in March of 2023, that when "Children tell us who they are,

---

37 Dyer, H. (2017). Queer futurity and childhood innocence: Beyond the injury of development. *Global Studies of Childhood*, 7(3), 290–302.

it is our job as grown-ups to listen and to believe them. That's what it means to be a good parent."[38] One can imagine the horror that follows from such a conviction—the idea that children can reason and consent as adults opens the door to "gender-affirming" life-altering surgeries. This conviction also opens the door to a very nasty corner of Queer Theory, where infamous Queer Activists like Gayle Rubin, writing in 1984, say things like:

> It is easy to see someone like Livingston as a victim of the child porn wars. It is harder for most people to sympathize with actual boy-lovers. Like communists and homosexuals in the 1950s, boylovers are so stigmatized that it is difficult to find defenders for their civil liberties, let alone for their erotic orientation. Consequently, the police have feasted on them. Local police, the FBI, and watchdog postal inspectors have joined to build a huge apparatus whose sole aim is to wipe out the community of men who love underaged youth. In twenty years or so, when some of the smoke has cleared, it will be much easier to show that these men have been the victims of a savage and undeserved witch hunt. A lot of people will be embarrassed by their collaboration with this persecution, but it will be too late to do much good for those men who have spent their lives in prison.[39] (Rubin, 1984/1993, p. 7)

The goal of a queer education is to "radically deconstruct" a child into a "fluid, permanently shifting, and unintelligible"[40] object

---

38   MSN. (2023, August 18). *Minnesota Lt. Gov. ripped for saying parents 'must believe' when kids 'tell us who they are'*. MSN. https://www.msn.com/en-us/news/us/minnesota-lt-gov-ripped-for-saying-parents-must-believe-when-kids-tell-us-who-they-are/ar-AA18ICrY

39   Rubin, G. S. (1984/1993). Thinking sex: Notes for a radical theory of the politics of sexuality. In H. Abelove, M. A. Barale, & D. M. Halperin (Eds.), *The lesbian and gay studies reader* (pp. 3–44). Routledge.

40   Luhmann, S. (1998). Queering/querying pedagogy? Or, pedagogy is a pretty

of revolution. Parents must understand what Queer Theory is doing to their children. Queer Activists know that parents will end the madness the second they realize their children are in danger, which is why Queer Activists intentionally subvert parental authority and teach children to expect parental rejection of their new "queer" identities. The zealots parading through our schools are doing everything they can to destroy the relationship parents have with their children. Queer Activists know they must eliminate the parent/child bond for the transformation to work.

Queer Activists have queered our schools, and our children now receive a *queer education*. It's time to understand what's going on so we can all stop the madness and restore the normalcy our children need to live happy, healthy, and fulfilling lives. It's time to understand Queer Theory.

---

queer thing. In W. F. Pinar (Ed.), *Queer Theory in education* (pp. 141–155). Lawrence Erlbaum Associates. (p. 124).

Chapter 2

WHAT IS
QUEER THEORY?

You would be hard-pressed to find a single K–12 school policy in the early 1990s that mentioned "gender identity" or "gender expression." You certainly wouldn't find any examples of teachers and administrators promoting "gender-neutral language" or "gender-affirming" policies and practices. The idea that schools could or should assist children in their quest to "transition" into a different sex or "gender" was unheard of back then.

A lot has changed. Today, Queer Activists, informed by Queer Theory, teach children that everyone has an inherent and fixed gender identity that society cannot question. They also teach children that "sex and gender are assigned at birth" and "sex and gender are social constructs." Our schools tell kids that society is designed to oppress them based on their sex, gender, and sexuality. They tell kids they can escape this unbearable situation by manufacturing a new *queer* identity for themselves. The

U.S. educational system now tells us we must acknowledge and celebrate our children's transformation.

What caused such a radical change in society's understanding of sex, gender, and sexuality in the last thirty years? Why are our schools saturated with such radicalism? In short—Queer Theory.

Queer Theory has a long history. Although it wasn't officially named and defined until the early 1990s, the intellectual tradition that gives Queer Theory its legs began, in earnest, in 1949. To understand what is happening in schools today, we must first travel back in time to understand where Queer Theory comes from, what it is, what it believes, and what it exists to do.

BORN IN PRISON

Contemporary scholars widely credit the French Marxist Simone de Beauvoir for paving the path for what would later become Queer Theory. Beauvoir's arguments, best articulated in her book *The Second Sex* (1949), introduced a distinction between sex and gender, decoupling biological reality from human behavior.

Beauvoir argued that men and women don't have an intrinsic nature (an *essence*). She claimed that biology in no way determines human behavior, attitudes, dispositions, or psychology. According to Beauvoir, the categories of "man" and "woman" are socially (read: politically) constructed. In her view, all observed differences between the behaviors of men and women resulted from social expectations and pressures designed to differentiate women as the inferior "second sex."

Beauvoir's argument can be best summarized in the most famous line of *The Second Sex*, "One is not born but becomes woman." In saying that "women" are *not born but made*, Beauvoir argues that social traditions and cultural norms determine what a "woman" is. In Beauvoir's view, society conditions girls into passive, nurturing, and subordinate roles to benefit men, whom society views as the primary and essential human beings. In other words, Beauvoir thought society defined what a "woman" should be and then pressured and groomed girls to become that thing. If a girl didn't fit society's mold, she would not be considered a "woman."

The idea that gender is a social construct will resonate with many people, especially feminists. History is filled with examples of women behaving differently in various societies and cultures, influenced by the varying expectations imposed upon and by them. If that is all Beauvoir argued, then we might not speak about her today. The core idea that Beauvoir advanced wasn't that some aspects of being a "proper" woman had been socially and politically regulated throughout history. Her core idea, which would become a central pillar upholding what would later become Queer Theory, is that "women" *do not exist* outside of political constructions. This isn't to say that Beauvoir thought females didn't exist. It is to say that Beauvoir thought that being a female *did not* make one a "woman."

> All agree in recognising the fact that females exist in the human species; today as always they make up about one half of humanity. And yet we are told that femininity is in danger; we are exhorted to be women, remain women, become women. It would appear, then, that every female human being is not necessarily a woman; to be so considered she must share in that mysterious and threatened reality known as femininity.[41] (de Beauvoir, 1949)

What began there shows up today in the Supreme Court. It is

---

41   de Beauvoir, S. (1949). *Introduction to the second sex.* Marxists Internet Archive.   https://www.Marxists.org/reference/subject/ethics/de-beauvoir/2nd-sex/introduction.htm

present behind the logic of Justice Gorsuch's decision about sex discrimination in transgender hiring and firing, and it is the direct causal beginning of now-Justice Ketanji Brown Jackson admitting before the United States Senate in her confirmation hearing that she couldn't answer the question "What is a woman?" despite being one. In drawing a distinction between a person's sex (biology) and their personality and behavior (what is called "gender"), Beauvoir turned "woman" into an empty category left to interpretation. This was a necessary step for her to take. If you're going to argue that women are unjustly defined on someone else's terms, then you must assume that the category of "woman" can be unlocked and defined by an outside influence in the first place. That is, you must first argue that women's behavior doesn't follow at all from their biology. If it did, even partially, a woman couldn't wholly redefine "woman" on her own terms.

In arguing that society makes women "the second sex," Beauvoir built herself a trap door to begin defining what a "woman" is differently. "Women...are the Other that is not self or subject, but object, because they do not define themselves; men define them," Beauvoir writes. If sex can remotely predict women's actions, then society, men, and women will always have something to point at to define women, thus "trapping" them. Beauvoir explicitly stated that female biology *imprisoned* women for this very reason.[42] In her view, a woman's ovaries and uterus were "peculiarities" that "circumscribe her within the limits of her own nature."[43] Put simply, Beauvoir was saying that men (and women) point to a woman's hips and boobs as a justification to treat her as a fallen form of human being. Beauvoir thought that "becoming" a woman was primarily a project of *breaking free from the prison of being born into a particular body*. Beauvoir had

---

42   ibid.
43   ibid.

to break the link between biology (sex) and personality/behavior (gender) completely for her arguments to hold.

In emptying the category of "woman," Beauvoir opened the door for females to define "woman" on their own terms *as women*. Beauvoir advocated for this approach exactly. She encouraged females to define themselves on their terms, outside of the external influence of both men and women. In this view, "woman" can't be defined *for* a female. It can only be defined *by* a female in an act of resistance against the prison of biology, society, and culture.

The thing is, as Justice Jackson showed the world, this ambition for women to self-determine at the most essential level is also a cult lie. Jackson replied that she couldn't answer the question because she is "not a biologist." There, she erred, but since she broadly represents the interests of the cult, she was granted a pass. Biology is not believed to determine the qualities of one's sex, so she named precisely the wrong kind of expert. In so doing, however, she generally indicated the right idea: *an expert* has to tell us what a woman is. The Queer Theory cult has seized that means of production in the intervening years. The inner-school cult adepts become the sex-and-gender gurus to whom we all must defer to decide when our sex and gender identification is legitimate, and their determination is that it is only real when it's aligned with Queer Cult activism. Beauvoir's legacy isn't the self-determination of women as women; it's handing the terms of the basis of that determination off to Queer Activists, i.e., radical cultists. Virtually all of trans activism and Queer Education follow.

THE PRISON WARDEN

Michel Foucault, a French communist who escaped allegations of pedophilia only in death, is widely considered the progenitor of

Queer Theory. Foucault's influence can't be overstated. He is one of the most cited researchers of all time, and contemporary Queer Theory publications are riddled with his name. Queer Activists use Foucault's ideas about power, knowledge, and normalcy as a lens through which they view and interpret society, sex, gender, and sexuality.

Foucault believed that there is *no objective truth* that humans have access to. For him, truth is a product of power, and power is a product of claiming "the truth." That is, truth and power are inseparable. In this view, everything society considers true is nothing more than what *has been made true* by those with the power to define and impose it. So, something becomes true because powerful people and institutions say it's true, just like how Queer Activists believe someone becomes "normal" because powerful people and institutions classify them as "normal." These powerful people and institutions then sell "the truth" back to society, convincing society to hand over more power to shape what "the truth" is. For Foucault, this "regime of truth" conserves the powerful interests of society.

Michel Foucault's *power/knowledge* thesis forwards a fundamentally different understanding of power than most people have. We generally consider power to operate from the top down, imposing its will from above, like a machine applying force. Foucault argued that this understanding is flawed, favoring the idea that power operates *through*, like electricity flowing through the grid. For him, institutions generate "regimes of truth" that trick people into believing that "the truth" is something we can determine at all. With a weight and air of legitimacy comes the power to decide which "truth" should be considered more valid and trustworthy. In this view, institutions don't directly force anyone to believe what is true, but they do shape tradition, norms, and values, which make it difficult for competing truth claims to gain recognition and legitimacy.

> Foucault, who is credited with laying the groundwork for much of Queer Theory, argues that discipline in (post)modernity creates "docile bodies," which conform to the discourses of capitalism, democracy, and the military-industrial complex. Rather than physical force coercing us to behave, surveillance of ourselves and one another propels us to act in accordance with these ruling discourses, for example, by conforming to rigid categorizations of gender and sexuality.[44] (Oswald & Kuvalanka & Blume & Berkowitz, 2009, p. 45)

In Foucault's worldview, the scientific disciplines are one of society's primary methods of controlling what "the truth" is. He believed that those in power saturate science with their subjective determinations and desires. That is, Foucault thought that science is not objective or neutral—it's a *subjective ideology* with no more valid claims to truth or knowledge than any other ideology that makes such claims. In this view, when scientific disciplines claim to know something, they aren't sharing *the truth*—they are selling a packaged product that those in power use to convince people to think or live in a certain way.

Foucault argued that the scientific disciplines used sexuality as a primary lever of human control. He believed that people in power had developed and used scientific disciplines to create an ideology of heterosexuality that tricks people into believing that heterosexual relationships are natural and normal. In this view, doctors and healthcare professionals, relying on the "validity" of

---

44 Oswald, R. F., Kuvalanka, K. A., Blume, L. B., & Berkowitz, D. (2009). Queering 'the family'. In S. A. Lloyd & A. L. Few (Eds.), *Handbook of feminist family studies* (pp. 43–55). SAGE Publications, Inc.

"the science," push people to conform to heterosexual relationships and lifestyles by deeming anything that strays from heterosexuality as deviant or abnormal.

In following this line of argumentation, doctors, psychiatrists, and other healthcare professionals push people into a belief system whereby those people internalize the norms of modern science and health. It's not just that the influential people determining what "real science looks like" are pushing their worldview onto people, imprisoning them in a system where no other "truths" about health and sexuality are permitted or validated. It's also that people, convinced by the authority of their healthcare institutions, *imprison themselves* by altering their bodies and sexual behaviors to conform to the dominant "truth" of heterosexuality. Indeed, Foucault's ideas about "the homosexual," as he termed it (read: "queer," according to David Halperin), follow directly from recycling Beauvoir's ideas about "woman."

Simone de Beauvoir and Michel Foucault introduced to those who would later name Queer Theory the idea that we are our own *prison wardens* but only because society expects us to be. It's not just that society tells us what to believe and how to behave. For Beauvoir and Foucault, we internalize these messages in our very being—our *soul*—and force our minds and bodies to adjust accordingly to conform to social expectations related to sex, gender, and sexuality. Under the constant threat of being labeled abnormal or deviant, our minds imprison our bodies, requiring them to act a certain way in the world.

THE QUEER LOCKSMITH

Gender Trouble is one of the most widely read works in Queer Theory. Published the same year that Teresa de Lauretis gave Queer Theory its name, the book builds on the works of Simone de Beauvoir and Michel Foucault to offer a "performative" view of sex, gender, and sexuality. The author, Judith Butler, grabs hold of Foucault's idea that "the soul is the prison of the body"[45] and offers Queer Activists a lock-pick, found in her theory of *gender performativity*.

Butler's chief argument is that "gender" is a performance. In fact, her entire argument could be succinctly summarized as "life is drag; drag is life." In *Gender Trouble*, Butler argues that people don't "have a gender." Instead, they "become a gender" through repeated acts and performances. That is, "Gender is not something that one is, it is something one does, a sequence of acts...a doing rather than a being."[46] Though she doesn't cite them. Butler is echoing the landmark gender studies paper by Candace West and Don H. Zimmerman from 1987 titled *Doing Gender*, which demonstrates how thoroughly these concepts were infused into radical (feminist) thought on sex, "gender," and sexuality in the 1980s and '90s.

Like Simone de Beauvoir and Michel Foucault, Butler argues that society created the categories of "men" and "women" for social control. In this view, society "scripts" the role of men and women and punishes anyone who doesn't *read their lines* correctly. Butler contends that everyone is born as a blank slate, and only by forcing people to read their predetermined lines do individuals "become" the character society scripts them to play. If a person happens to be born with a vagina and uterus, then "she" will be expected to "become a woman" by learning "her" role and playing it correctly. If a person happens to be born with a penis, then "he" will be expected to "become a man" through learning "his" role and playing it correctly. Society writes the script and

45   Butler, J. (1990). *Gender trouble: Feminism and the subversion of identity*. Routledge. (p. 172).
46   Mikkola, M. (2008). *Feminist perspectives on sex and gender*. Stanford Encyclopedia of Philosophy

socializes people into playing their part with rewards and punishments coded in for good and bad performances.

Butler suggests that individuals can become conscious of the fact that what society considers "gender" is nothing more than an *act of theater*. In becoming conscious, individuals can begin to *act differently* in an attempt to call attention to the fact that everyone is taking part in a stage play. For Butler, the more the act of gender departs from the "normal," the better. When a highly sexualized man dawns on a colorful dress, wig, and lipstick, it shocks people. The shock of drag performances mocks the idea of stable gender categories because men can transcend boundaries and "become" women.

Like the drag queen, Butler argues that transgender individuals call into question "gender reality." According to Butler, some transgender individuals are so convincing that onlookers "cannot with surety ready the body that one sees," and this is "precisely the moment when one is no longer sure whether the body encountered is that of a man or a woman."

> When such categories come into question, the reality of gender is also put into crisis: it becomes unclear how to distinguish the real from the unreal. And this is the occasion in which we come to understand that what we take to be "real," what we invoke as the naturalized knowledge of gender is, in fact, a changeable and revisable reality.[47] (Butler, 1990, p. xxiii)

If "gender reality" is revisable, then so too is biological reality. According to Butler, Simone de Beauvoir "certainly la[id] the groundwork"[48] for this view. Butler suggests that the leap from

---

47   Butler, J. (1990). *Gender trouble: Feminism and the subversion of identity.* Routledge.
48   Butler, J. (1986). Sex and Gender in Simone de Beauvoir's Second Sex. Yale

"gender is a social construct" to "sex is also a social construct" was ultimately facilitated through the radicalization of Beauvoir's work specifically and the radicalization of feminism more broadly, with significant contributions from Monique Wittig and Michel Foucault. Building on her intellectual inheritance, Butler's theory of gender performativity inaugurated the complete dismantling of sex. When sex is decoupled from personality and behavior (gender), then sex, as Butler suggests, loses all meaning.

> If the immutable character of sex is contested, perhaps this construct called "sex" is as culturally constructed as gender; indeed, perhaps it was always already gender, with the consequence that the distinction between sex and gender turns out to be no distinction at all.[49] (Butler, 1990, p. 10)

It's not hard to follow this line of logic. If sex doesn't determine anything about how we behave or think, then it doesn't matter in determining who we are. If sex is just biology, but that biology doesn't affect our personality or behavior, then individuals just *happen to be born in* "sexed bodies," left to perform and determine their "gender" on their own accord. But these "sexed bodies," in this line of logic, don't have any meaning outside their ability to reproduce. They do not signify being a "man" or a "woman." They only signify flesh and bone. If they don't represent anything other than flesh and bone, then any traits we ascribe to them are nothing more than political constructions, just like gender. A "pure body," according to Butler, "cannot be found."[50] "What can be found is the situated body, a locus of cultural interpretations."

French Studies, (72), 35–49. Yale University Press.

49 Butler, J. (1990). *Gender trouble: Feminism and the subversion of identity.* Routledge.

50 Butler, J. (1986). Sex and Gender in Simone de Beauvoir's Second Sex. Yale French Studies, (72), 35–49. Yale University Press.

Put simply, Butler suggests we just happen to be born in a body that looks and works one way or the other. Sex, in this sense, is an allusion—it only becomes discernible through cultural interpretations of anatomical differences and does not mean anything prior to such interpretations.[51]

Butler, like many infected by Critical Marxism and Postmodernism, is particularly pessimistic about this state. She does not believe that the socialization of "normal" society can be entirely broken, so she recommends a particular and passive-aggressive approach to Queer Activism: *the politics of parody*. What this means is that Butler's Queer Theory encourages using parodies of gender, sex, and sexual stereotypes as a wedge to undermine people's belief in them. Following from this are drag, the "camp" aesthetic, and even the leaning into gender stereotypes as definitional at the heart of trans presentation, either through strategic exaggeration or intentional gender-bending, like a bearded lady. The goal of this approach is to mock the meaning out of sex, gender, and sexuality entirely to undermine people's belief in them as meaningful and stable categories relevant to being. In the end, everyone becomes queer because no one can believe in "normal" anymore.

For Butler, choosing to perform your gender (or sex!) differently than how society scripts you to do so isn't just a way to get a few laughs in a feeble attempt to *give it to the Patriarchy*! Performing your gender differently is an act of freeing your *soul*. This is the most important takeaway from Butler's writing. If we can tolerate and toil over her infamously awful prose, the purpose of Queer Theory—what it's meant to do when practiced—becomes clear. Butler writes:

---

51   ibid.

The figure of the interior soul understood as "within" the body is signified through its inscription on the body, even though its primary mode of signification is through its very absence, its potent invisibility. The effect of a structuring inner space is produced through the signification of a body as a vital and sacred enclosure. The soul is precisely what the body lacks; hence, the body presents itself as a signifying lack. That lack which is the body signifies the soul as that which cannot show. In this sense, then, the soul is a surface signification that contests and displaces the inner/outer distinction itself, a figure of interior psychic space inscribed on the body as a social signification that perpetually renounces itself as such. In Foucault's terms, the soul is not imprisoned by or within the body, as some Christian imagery would suggest, but "the soul is the prison of the body.[52] (Butler, 1990, p. 172)

I know. *Awful.* Anyway, what Butler is suggesting here, as did Foucault, is that our bodies are a reflection of our souls—our divine, if you will, consciousness. If you combine this view with Butler and Foucault's idea that our consciousness is *socially determined and imposed*, then you're left with a terrifying conclusion—*your body* is a political construction wielded by those in power to maintain their status, privilege, and control. Queer Theory holds that you build your body into a prison for your soul because society at large puts constraints on what you can and should do with your body. Thus, the soul (of society) imprisons the body, which in turn imprisons the real *you* that has to live in it. Queer Theory's status as a gnostic religious cult is hardly more visible anywhere than here, in its most basic assumptions.

The general argument forwarded by Queer Theory today, following the works of Beauvoir, Foucault, and Butler, goes like

---

52 Butler, J. (1990). *Gender trouble: Feminism and the subversion of identity.* Routledge.

this: Society brainwashes us to think about the world in specific ways. Political constructions (Queer Theory's *evil spirits*), conjured by those in power, bombard our souls with "the truth" of the world. Our souls, possessed by political constructions, then command our bodies to act—to perform—in accordance with the scripts society is writing for us. *We make our souls— our "divine" consciousness—material on our bodies.* We materialize society's traditions, norms, and values on our physical, fallen forms. We then look in the mirror, and our body—now taking the form of society's powerful political interests—reflects back on our soul, making it think, "This is who I am—I am a man/ woman." But you are not yourself. You are wholly alienated from who you really are. *Society is convincing you to alienate and imprison yourself.*

Following from this, the goal of Queer Theory is to break the brainwashing program so you can free yourself *from yourself (as society allegedly demands you to be).* The goal is to break off the societal chains on your soul so you can realize who you really are "on the inside." To do this, you start *queering* society, breaking all traditions, rules, and norms. Then, free from the constraints of an illegitimate order, you *become queer.*

WHAT IS QUEER THEORY?

To answer the question of what Queer Theory is, I will give two brief answers in this chapter and a far longer, more in–depth answer in the next chapter.

THE SHORT ANSWER

Queer Theory is a radical ideology that uses activism (*queering*) to convince people that nothing is normal or natural. It specializes in convincing people that sex, gender, and sexuality are social (political) constructs—fabrications invented and sold as "the truth" by dominant classes—but those categories are not limiting factors. Queer Theory's activity is to *deconstruct* the very concept of normalcy. The result is that Queer Activists put themselves in the position of determining what is and is not a "valid" way of being, which they enforce negatively by criticizing everything that disagrees with Queer Activism and encourage positively by affirming and celebrating anything that advances Queer Activism. "*What is a woman?*" It's whatever and whomever—and *only* whatever and whomever—Queer Activists say it is.

Queer Theory broadly argues that society is a prison constructed by dominant classes who artificially label some things as "normal," "legitimate," or "true" for their own benefit. More specifically, Queer Theory argues that the prison the dominant classes create convinces people that they must live, act, and behave in specific ways. Under the weight of this conviction, people *imprison their bodies*, adopting specific behavioral patterns, styles of dress, and sexual preferences in accordance with what the dominant classes tell them is "normal."

The goal of Queer Theory is to use political activism to make people conscious of the "prison" society locks us all into, thereby making people conscious of the prison they have constructed for themselves. This *queer consciousness* is the state of being awake to the "truth" of Queer Theory. In developing a queer consciousness, one becomes a radical activist who uses Queer Theory as the lens through which they view all of society. Queer Theory informs how those with queer consciousness think and act in the world. Queer consciousness inspires one to view society as a prison they must dismantle and break free from to *free their soul*. In short, Queer Theory is a vehicle for a complete and perpetual cultural and personal *revolution*.

THE MEDIUM ANSWER

Queer Theory adopts the idea that cultural norms and science, an institution that includes biology, medicine, and psychiatry, are used by dominant classes to determine what a "normal" man, woman, and sexuality are. These dominant classes define themselves as normal, situating themselves in opposition to those they have deemed abnormal and deviant. In creating categories of "normal people" and "abnormal people," and of "legitimate ways of being" and "deviant ways of being," dominant classes construct a hierarchy of power where they are privileged. They use this position as a pillar of legitimacy to tell *all* people how they must live and act.

Queer Theory believes that the power structure that emerges from dominant classes determining how society should look—and to whom society must grant privilege—is hidden under cover of various ideologies. These ideologies hide the power dynamics of society from both the dominant and oppressed classes. That is to say, these ideologies blind everyone to the actual workings of power in society, convincing everyone—normal and abnormal—that the way society is structured is neutral, balanced, and fair. Ideology, in other words, stabilizes the system by making society appear as if it is normal and natural to organize itself in the way that it has.

Queer Theory has named "heteronormativity" as one such ideology. According to Queer Theory, "heteronormative ideology refers to the belief that there are two separate and opposing genders with associated natural roles that match their assigned sex, and that heterosexuality is a given."[53]

---

53   van der Toorn, J., Pliskin, R., & Morgenroth, T. (2020). Not quite over the rainbow: The unrelenting and insidious nature of heteronormative ideology. *Current Opinion in Behavioral Sciences*, 34, 160–165.

Heteronormativity is an ideological code that promotes rigidly defined conventional gender norms, heterosexuality, and "traditional family values." Current social and intimate experiences are defined by a heterosexual/homosexual binary that serves as a method of social control to encourage conformity within the heteronormative power structure. Heteronormativity has very real material consequences for those situated differently in the matrix of domination. Queer scholarship questions how institutionalized heterosexuality ensures that some people will have more power, privilege, status, and resources than others.[54] (Oswald & Kuvalanka & Blume & Berkowitz, 2009, p. 45)

Queer Theory believes that "heteronormativity" uses science as cover for a political project to justify the idea that a person is either a man or a woman and that it is normal for men and women to be attracted to the opposite sex. That is to say, Queer Theory thinks that heterosexual people have unjustly defined themselves as "normal" to position themselves on top of a power hierarchy that they weave into the very fabric of society. Queer Theory explicitly argues that there is no such thing as normal sexuality, and any justification rooted in biology or science is a "fake fact" used to control people.

Another ideology that Queer Theory believes is ubiquitous is "cisgender" ideology or "cisnormativity." Cisgender ideology is the idea that an individual's gender must match their "sex assigned at birth." Queer Theory believes that cisgender ideology brainwashes people to think that one's sex determines their gender, forcing males to identify as men and females to identify as women. In this view, "cisgender" people have created society and

---

54   Oswald, R. F., Kuvalanka, K. A., Blume, L. B., & Berkowitz, D. (2009). Queering 'the family'. In S. A. Lloyd & A. L. Few (Eds.), *Handbook of feminist family studies* (pp. 43–55). SAGE Publications, Inc.

unjustly labeled themselves as normal to position themselves on top of the power hierarchy.

Often, Queer Activists reference the two ideologies together in "cisheteronormativity." The same formula applies. Cisheteronormativity is the belief that straight people who identify with their sex assigned at birth have created society, unjustly labeling themselves as "normal" to exclude and oppress everyone that isn't "cisheterosexual."

In addition, Queer Theory defines another ideology called "homonormativity," which doesn't mean what it sounds like it means. "Homonormativity" is an ideology that brainwashes people—especially homosexual people—to believe being gay or lesbian is or can be normal, as opposed to intrinsically radical. It convinces people—especially homosexual people—to believe gay and lesbian people should be accepted as a normal variation of human sexuality and even to "pass" by dressing and living their lives in ways Queer Activists deem to be "coded as" "normal," what might be described paradoxically as "the straight people of gay people." Queer Activists believe being gay or lesbian should be a front of radical potential and Queer Activism, not just another normal variation of human experience, and so they believe the adoption of "homonormativity" further oppresses "queer" people by normalizing homosexuality.

Queer Theory argues that "normal people" design all of society to brainwash people's *souls*. Queer Theory claims that social constructions of sex, gender, and sexuality convince people that they are "men" and "women." Convinced of this, "men" and "women" alter their bodies and behaviors to reflect the social constructions that are impressed upon them. In this view, society brainwashes women into making their bodies appear more feminine, whereas society brainwashes men into making their bodies appear more masculine. Women force their behavior to be more "ladylike," and men force their behavior to be more "manly." Likewise, Queer Theory claims that society brainwashes men and women into believing they must participate in heterosexual relationships and brainwashes gays and lesbians into "passing" as straight by living normal lives. By breaking the social constructions of sex, gender, and sexuality—by breaking *society*—Queer Theory believes it is freeing people's *souls*, thus freeing them to act, appear, and behave differently—that is, *queerly*.

The goal of Queer Theory is to awaken people to the "truth" of Queer Theory; to brainwash people into believing that there is no such thing as a "normal" man, woman, gender, sexuality, or society. In fact, the goal is to advance the idea that there is no such thing as "normal" at all. They, themselves, become the *de facto* arbiters of what is and isn't "valid" expression in the vacuum created by this deconstructive perspective.

A person who has accepted the truth of Queer Theory has developed a queer consciousness. A person with a queer consciousness is *queer*. Queer, as defined in the Queer Theory literature, is a radical political identity—it is, as we saw, "whatever is at odds with the normal, the legitimate, the dominant."[55]

Those with queer consciousness work to break the prison of society by agitating for social change. Collectively, *queers* use radical activism to break things. In their mind, they are breaking chains to free their minds so they can "become" whoever they feel they are. In reality, they are breaking the very things that make civilization possible. Queer Activists are narcissists who want the world to bend to their will, and they think that anything that tells them "No" must be destroyed. Queer Theory is a dangerous, destructive cult religion.

---

55   Halperin, D. M. (1995). *Saint Foucault: Towards a gay hagiography*. Oxford University Press. (p. 62).

Chapter 3

QUEER THEORY, A.K.A QUEER MARXISM

Simone de Beauvoir, Michel Foucault, and Judith Butler didn't develop their theories of sex, gender, and sexuality from scratch. Each of these thinkers shares a common philosophical starting point—a framework that they mapped their ideas about sex, gender, and sexuality onto. If Queer Theory is a vehicle for cultural and personal revolution, it runs on the engine of Marxism. In fact, Queer Theory is *Queer Marxism*. Queer Theory cannot be understood without peeking under the hood, revealing the Marxist mechanics that give it life.

THE MORE PRECISE ANSWER

Marxism is predicated on the idea that Man is "creative" and "social" in nature. For Marx, those are the things that make us human. In his *Economic and Philosophic Manuscripts of 1844*, Marx argues that humans differentiate themselves from animals by making their "life activity itself the object of [their] will and [their] consciousness." In other words, Marx argued that animals just live in the world—their existence is an existence driven by their instincts. Animals plug into their environment, and their environment contours and shapes their "life activity." Humans, on the other hand, are transformers of their environment. We contour and shape the world around us.

For Marx, being "creative" means that humans are born in the world—in nature—and we consciously decide what we want that world to look like. Then, we get to work, transforming nature by making the things we are inspired to make. But, for Marx, we're not only transforming nature by making things like spears, baskets, and skyscrapers—we're also *making ourselves*. Marx argues that we make ourselves through our work on the world. We take our consciousness and make it an object. The thoughts in our head become material—we materialize them.

> It is just in his work upon the objective world, therefore, that man really proves himself to be a species-being. This production is his active species-life. Through this production, nature appears as his work and his reality. The object of labor is, therefore, the objectification of man's species-life: for he duplicates himself not only, as in consciousness, intellectually, but also actively, in reality, and therefore he sees himself in a world that he has created.[56] (Marx, 1844)

An example might help us better understand Marx's proclamation that Man "sees himself in a world that he has created." For instance, I might see a tree branch on the ground and think, "I want to make a spear." I envision what my spear looks like and

---

56   Marx, K. (1844). *Economic and Philosophic Manuscripts of 1844*. Marxists Internet Archive. https://www.Marxists.org/archive/marx/works/1844/manuscripts /preface.htm

set out to transform the tree branch I've found into that vision. I take a nearby sharp rock and begin shaving away. I cut at the branch, removing its bark and carving away at it until I have a sharp point on one side. Now I have a spear. I've taken the image in my head and labored on nature to materialize that vision.

After making my spear, I step back and look at it. What do I see? I see a spear—of course. But what I really see is *myself.* Through working on nature, I have materialized my consciousness, and by reflecting on my creation I come to know myself as a creator. In that reflection, I fulfill what makes me different from animals—in being creative, I come to know myself as human. Creativity is part of my nature, and each time I make something in the world, I become more human, and the world becomes more human because I'm putting more of myself—my thoughts turned material—into the world. I'm transforming the world into me. The world and I are becoming one and the same through my "conscious life activity." The distinction between myself and nature is evaporating. I'm *humanizing* the world, and each time I do it, I more fully realize who I am.

Humans aren't born into a vacuum. For Marx, we inherit a world that previous generations have already worked on. This means that each of us is born into a nature that has already, in part, been humanized by the "dead generations" that weigh "like a nightmare" on our brains. In Marx's own words:

> Men make their own history, but they do not make it as they please; they do not make it under self-selected circumstances, but under circumstances existing already, given and transmitted from the past. The tradition of all dead generations weighs like a nightmare on the brains of the living. And just as they seem to be occupied with revolutionizing themselves and things, creating something that did not exist before, precisely in such epochs of revolutionary crisis

they anxiously conjure up the spirits of the past to their service, borrowing from them names, battle slogans, and costumes in order to present this new scene in world history in time-honored disguise and borrowed language.[57] (Marx, 1852)

We're born into a world of our contemporaries, each working on nature. Therefore, the world we're born into reflects a certain level of humanity back onto our consciousness. This reflection *determines* our range of thoughts and experiences, thus affecting our *creative* potential. If I'm born into a primitive tribe, I'm not going to build the space station. I only have the history of my tribe's work in and on the world to draw from. For Marx, the history of my tribe's work preloads my consciousness. In this sense, I am my tribe. I don't think as an individual in a vacuum. There is no "I think," only "we think." Marx thought consciousness is social—you affect what I think, and I affect what you think. Both directly and through our work, we make not only ourselves but also each other. We are one thing—the species Man. That is, Marx thought humans were naturally *collectivists*.

Karl Marx thought that we are a creative species that humanizes the world so we can come to know ourselves as Man. In this view, Man makes society, and society reflects Man's image back onto him. That is, humans create a society, and that society then conditions future humans in the image of those who originally made it. Marx called these activities "praxis" (man makes society) and "the inversion of praxis" (society socializes, thus makes, man)—a circle, that in the words of Hegel "runs back into itself, presupposing the beginning it reaches in the end." We collectively work on nature and create a society, and that society reflects the history of our progress back onto us. Unlike the animals, *we*

57 Marx, K. (1852). *The Eighteenth Brumaire of Louis Bonaparte*. Marxists Internet Archive. https://www.Marxists.org/archive/marx/works/1852/18th-brumaire

make history and are at the same time *the products of the history we continually make.* Unlike the animals, we can therefore *seize the means of production* of history and thus of ourselves.

For Marx, the march to realize our humanity progresses inevitably. Eventually, we'll reach the end of History when we have transformed nature to such an extent that it is indistinguishable from us. Man will be nature, and nature will be man. When we look out and into the world, the only thing reflecting back at us will be our creativity—the only thing reflecting back on us will be ourselves. Our collectivized consciousness will become one with itself. What's in our heads will already reflect back at us in the world—all we will think and see is *We are Man, Creator.* History will end because we will have realized our full human nature as creative and collective beings. We will, collectively, become God, and in so doing we will remember that we were already God and have been all along. As Marx himself suggests in his *Critique of Hegel's Philosophy of Right*, the goal of critiquing all other religions is to make way for Man to move around himself as his own true Sun:

> The criticism of religion disillusions man, so that he will think, act, and fashion his reality like a man who has discarded his illusions and regained his senses, so that he will move around himself as his own true Sun. Religion is only the illusory Sun which revolves around man as long as he does not revolve around himself. (Marx, 1844, p. 1)

This is the *theology of Marxism*, which defines a transformative, collectivist gnostic cult.

THE FALL OF MAN

If you've heard anything about Marxism at all, you've likely heard that Marx said capitalism is bad because it allows wealthy business owners to steal "surplus value" from their workers. That is, Marx thought it was unfair that some people make products for business owners who then take those products and sell them for a profit. After all, "The worker is doing the work!" Marx did think this, but he thought this for a specific reason. Marx thought that business owners *alienated workers from their labor*. This *estranged* labor turns:

> Man's species-being, both nature and his spiritual species-property, into a being alien to him…It estranges from man his own body, as well as external nature and his spiritual aspect, his human aspect. An immediate consequence of the fact that man is estranged from the product of his labor, from his life activity, from his species-being, is the estrangement of man from man.[58] (Marx, 1844)

Marx's "economic" arguments cannot be reduced to "capitalism isn't fair because some people work for slave wages while others get rich." His economic arguments follow from his theology. Man is already a "species-being," a completely social and socialist self-creative entity, but estranged labor makes his true nature as such "alien to him." That is, capitalism makes man forget who he really is: a (perfect) socialist. In the terminology of gnostic cults, "socialism" is the hidden self-knowledge, or gnosis, that enables the path toward salvation.

Marx therefore thought that capitalism must go because the division of labor literally *makes us animals* pitted against one another. Remember, Marxist theology argues that we are only human if we are "creative" and "social." If someone *forces me* to make the thoughts *in their head*—their products, their

---

58   Marx, K. (1844). *Economic and Philosophic Manuscripts of 1844.* Marxists Internet Archive. https://www.Marxists.org/archive/marx/works/1844/manuscripts /preface.htm

services—a reality *for them*, then that person is denying *my* humanity. They are *alienating me from myself* because my labor no longer "belong[s] to [my] intrinsic nature."[59] In the process, they alienate the whole species because the species lives in each of us. Put simply, the division of labor—where one man owns the business and the other works for wages—is the *Fall of Man* in the gnostic Marxist theology.

In the Judeo-Christian tradition, Adam and Eve disobeyed God and ate from the Tree of Knowledge of Good and Evil in the Garden of Eden. Their actions flung them into a world filled with sin, misery, and death. In the theology of Marxism, Man ate from the Tree of Knowledge of Good and Evil in nature and learned that he could *own private property* and upon that ownership divide his labor, which alienates him from himself as a creative and social species. In his fallen form, estranged from his species-being (his humanity), he finds himself in a society stratified into classes, which leads to conflict, exploitation, misery, and oppression. To re-enter (and, in fact, re-create) the kingdom of God—Man's kingdom on Earth—he must establish a communist society by abolishing *private property*, which is nothing more than *materialized* "human self-estrangement."

> Communism as the positive transcendence of private property as human self-estrangement, and therefore as the real appropriation of the human essence by and for man; communism therefore as the complete return of man to himself as a social (i.e., human) being – a return accomplished consciously and embracing the entire wealth of previous development. This communism, as fully developed naturalism, equals humanism, and as fully developed humanism equals naturalism; it is the genuine resolution of the conflict between man and nature and between man and man – the true resolution

---

59   ibid.

of the strife between existence and essence, between objectification and self-confirmation, between freedom and necessity, between the individual and the species. Communism is the riddle of history solved, and it knows itself to be this solution.[60] (Marx, 1844)

Marx was not an economist or social theorist. He was a theologian in a revolutionary gnostic faith who mapped "economics" and "social theory" onto his theology to sell it. When Marx wrote about centralizing "all instruments of production in the hands of the State,"[61] he wasn't referencing economic production. Marx was referencing the *production of Man*. As a gnostic cult, Marx's theology would hold that those with the power of production in society *build* society, which would make them the "Demiurge" (builder, creator, artisan, but also prison warden) for Man in that society. Marxism is therefore, as a religion, the aim to seize control of demiurgic power, to become not God but the Socialist Demiurge who, upon completing his task of undoing the Fall of Man, would liberate humanity through an act of self-sacrifice, thus actualizing himself fully as (Socialist) God.

The communist revolution Marx called for needed to capture full State power so the communists could, in their eyes, "humanize" Man and complete the gnostic liberation. Marx wanted socialists to take control of the State (become the Demiurge who builds society) because he believed that the State conditions and limits Man's *creativity*. By creating a socialist State through socialist praxis, you create a Socialist Man through the inversion of praxis—through "the circle that runs back into itself, presupposing the beginning it reaches in the end." As people

---

60   ibid.
61   Marx, K., & Engels, F. (1848). *The Communist Manifesto*. Retrieved from https://www.Marxists.org/archive/marx/works/1848/communist-manifesto/ch02.htm

adopt more socialist beliefs (become Socialist Elect), so the argument goes, those people would work to perfect the socialist State, which in turn would perfect the socialist attitudes of future generations. That this happens through carceral (demiurgic) State power is no problem because power is always carceral and the ends of liberation justify the means of totalitarianism to get Man to realize himself as his fully social self. Marxism argues that the cycle of *Man makes society and society makes Man* eventually ends when Man fully realizes his creative and social nature. At that point, the State is no longer necessary because Man has realized his full humanity. The State—*the divine savior*—sacrifices itself and withers away. Viola! Communism. That is, the "real Communism" that has never been tried. The spoiler is that it will never be tried because it is a religious artifact of a theology based on impossible circular logic.

QUEER MARXIST THEOLOGY

Millions of dead bodies bear witness to the fact that Marxism doesn't work. Marxism doesn't work because it's not an economic or social theory. Marxism is a cult theology, so acting as if it has anything to do with economics produces devastating consequences. But that has never stopped Marxists from believing in the promises of Marxism. When "classical" or "vulgar" Marxism was revealed to be a catastrophic failure, Marxists simply tweaked Marxism to account for an ever-increasing series of variables and excuses. Losing Marxism meant losing the promise of salvation. The cult of Marxism just couldn't let it go.

For instance, the Marxists of the early 20th century struggled to understand why communist revolutions weren't taking hold in precisely the places Marx predicted they would. People in highly industrial societies were not developing the "class consciousness" required to kick-start the bloodshed. Defeated, these Marxists critiqued and updated Marxism. Cultural and Critical Marxism was born from this critique, arguing that Western culture subdued class consciousness. Whereas Marx thought capitalism's contradictions would inevitably catalyze a revolution when working conditions became too brutal to bear, Cultural and Critical Marxists theorized that this was not possible. Western cultural institutions, they argued, used spoon-fed values and cultural norms to brainwash people into believing that capitalism was good for them. In fact, by the 1960s, Critical Marxists like Herbert Marcuse and Max Horkheimer were admitting that "advanced capitalism" "delivers the good" and "allows [workers] to build a better life," one "to be sure" is a "good life." This, they observed, robbed the working class of its revolutionary energy and potential by stabilizing the worker in his good life. In other words, the communist revolution was no longer inevitable; the worker was no longer likely to be its vehicle; and Marxists needed new tools to push us all towards the end of History. Marcuse, following the success of Mao's Chinese revolution, suggested identity politics would be the place to turn.

Queer Theory's most influential contributors were all Marxist in orientation. Simone de Beauvoir, Michel Foucault, and Judith Butler inherited the core concepts developed by Marxists in the first half of the 20th century and applied them specifically to studying sex, gender, and sexuality. They used Marxist theology as a launchpad for their social critiques and, in so doing, created the new flavor of Marxism that we are all dealing with today—Queer Marxism.

The basic structure of "classical" Marxism looks like this: Society is stratified between a demiurgic dominant class—the Bourgeoisie—and an oppressed class—the Proletariat. This stratification places these classes in direct conflict with one another. The Bourgeoisie have risen to and maintain their dominant position in society by creating *the idea of private property (capital)* and taking it for themselves, resulting in the alienation of Man from his true and salvific socialist nature. The Bourgeoisie couches their justification for why they have private property—and others do not—in an ideology called *capitalism*. Capitalism brainwashes people to believe that organizing society based on who has private property and who doesn't is normal, common sense, and fair. Capitalism coerces *everyone* to believe that "this is just how the world works." It is incumbent on the oppressed class to become conscious of "the truth" of Marxism—to develop a *class consciousness* and adopt *socialism*—and to become revolutionaries charged with taking control of society and abolishing (transcending) private property as a form of human self-estrangement. In abolishing private property, Man returns to his creative and social nature (communism).

Queer Theory was built on top of the "classical" Marxist structure: Society is stratified between a demiurgic dominant class—"normal people"—and an oppressed class—"abnormal people." This stratification places these classes in direct conflict with one another. Normal people have risen to and maintain their dominant position in society by creating *the idea of private sociocultural property*—"being normal" or "normalcy"—and then taking that private property for themselves, resulting in the alienation of Man from his true and salvific queer nature. Normal people couch their justification for why they are considered "normal" and others are not in an ideology called *normativity* (broadly) *and cisheteronormativity* (specifically). The ideology of *normativity* brainwashes people to believe that organizing society based on who is considered "normal" and who is not is common sense, natural, and fair. The ideology of *normativity* coerces everyone to believe that "this is just how the world works." It is incumbent on the oppressed class—"abnormal people"—to become conscious of "the truth" of Queer Theory—to develop a *queer consciousness*—and to become revolutionaries charged with taking control of society and abolishing (transcending) "normalcy" as a form of human self-estrangement. In abolishing normalcy, Man returns to his creative and social nature, which is intrinsically queer.

Karl Marx's revolutionary theory of History aimed to radicalize people and encourage them to take control of society, forcing everything and everyone to become communist. Queer Marxism is no different. Queer Marxism's revolutionary theory of History aims to radicalize people, encourage them to take control of society, and force everything and everyone to become *queer*.

Queer, as David Halperin writes, "need not be grounded in any positive truth or in any stable reality. As the very word implies, 'queer' does not name some natural kind or refer to some determinate object; it acquires its meaning from its oppositional relation to the norm. Queer is by definition *whatever* is at odds with the normal, the legitimate, the dominant. There is *nothing in particular to which it necessarily refers*. It is an identity without an essence."[62] If we take this definition and recall the contributions of Simone de Beauvoir, Michel Foucault, and Judith Butler, the picture becomes crystal clear. Queer Theory is Queer Marxism, which means Queer Theory is Queer Marxist Theology. Queer Theory is the study of what we might call "*Queer* Divinity," rather than Man's Divinity. Thus we make sense of statements that are commonplace today like "trans people are sacred."

Queer Theory argues that sex and gender are social constructs—demiurgic political categories created by powerful people and institutions to oppress everyone. These political categories form an ideology that tells everyone that it's normal to "identify"

---

62 Halperin, D. M. (1995). *Saint Foucault: Towards a gay hagiography*. Oxford University Press. (p. 62).

as a man or woman attracted to the opposite sex. The ideology of "normativity" conditions people to act a certain way so the oppressors can maintain and expand their power and privileges.

First, Simone de Beauvoir drew a sharp distinction between sex and gender. She said "women" are definitely females, but that biology only affects them insofar as others say it does. In other words, a person is born either male or female, but none of their personalities or behaviors follow from their sex. What does this mean? Gender exists and is entirely a construct of political power.

Foucault expanded Beauvoir's analysis of the category of "woman" to include other categories, like "homosexual." He argued that the scientific disciplines aren't neutral, objective, or fair. For him, there is no universal truth in the world that humans have access to. The scientific method is bunk, he says, just another unjust application of dominant power. So, the oppressors in society take "their science" and tell everyone that it's objective so they can mold you into a normal person—so they can control how you identify—control what your sex, gender, and sexuality are. The administrative team asks me to circle "man" or "woman" at the doctor's office. Everyone assumes the stranger they meet at the bus stop is straight. Society tells us, "That's not normal!" when we step out of line, which conditions us to start acting normal—how we should act to keep society functioning *normally.*

After Beauvoir and Foucault, Judith Butler, the queen of Queer Theory, argues that we don't have a gender—we *perform* our gender. That is, when we act in the world, that action reflects back on us and society *as gender.* So, gender is something you do; something you construct; it manifests itself in action. How *creative!*

Queer Theory argues that the "soul is the prison of the body." That is, the nature we're born into reflects a bunch of images of what a man or woman should be, what our sexuality should be, and how we should behave and dress. These reflections condition our subjective thoughts—our creativity. Our creativity then makes that conditioning *a material reality on our bodies.* Our soul, as a part of the broader social "soul" of the present society, imprisons our bodies. We are thrown into a world where sex, gender, and sexuality are entirely fake products of a political power that tells us we must conform. Those constructs condition our soul—our "gender identity," or our *gender soul*—which in turn imprisons our bodies in a particular material form.

The goal of Queer Theory is to become conscious of this by breaking the conditioning on our soul. The goal is to develop a revolutionary queer consciousness. This consciousness slowly casts off the political conditions that are "scripted" onto our souls, convincing us to script our bodies. Developing a queer consciousness is the process of casting off the chains to free our souls completely. The goal is to realize our true "gender identity" or "gender soul" for what it really is, which is whatever our feelings tell us it is.

To return to the point, you sometimes see the phrase "trans people are sacred" on billboards or social media. The phrase isn't hyperbole. In Queer Theory, trans people are considered sacred because they have developed a queer consciousness. They have cast off the chains, revealing their true "gender soul." They are now free to turn their subjective thoughts into material reality. They can now literally "become women" or "become men" on *their terms.* Queer Activists won't let you escape this point—a trans person is whatever they say they are because they are considered *divine.*

Queer Theory argues that there is no such thing as a man or a woman, biologically or not. We're just born in a body that *happens to have* a penis or a vagina, or specific chromosomes, or a particular genetic code. In this sense:

people with both beards and breasts, people with penises who also menstruate, people with hormone levels that are usually associated with other genitalia and people with ambiguous genitalia, are considered to exist beyond the range of normal sexual development. Nevertheless, all of these primary and secondary sex characteristics, and their various combinations, occur naturally on a continuum. It is human society, not biology, that determines the categorical difference between a large clitoris and a small penis, how much hair a woman should have and where, and the difference between female breasts and a male chest...sex and gender are both social constructs.[63] (DePalma, 2013, p. 5)

Queer Theory doesn't care about biology, science, or truth—those things are all controlled by the "normal" Bourgeoisie—the ruling class. This ruling class alienates people, collecting this alienation as material power to impose their worldview and way of life on everyone else under the guise of "being normal." If private property is the material form of "human self-estrangement" in Marxist Theology, then "normalcy" is a form of private property, the material form of "human self-estrangement" in Queer Marxist Theology.

When the doctor observes a penis and "assigns the male sex" to a person at birth, they alienate that person from deciding what "sex" they are for themselves. This alienation manifests in "normalcy." That is, the doctor, through her meticulous and supremely difficult(!) observation of human genitalia at birth, is stealing a person's agency to determine their sex and gender for themselves. If the rest of the professionals in the doctor's practice also decide to "assign sex at birth," they can pool this

---

63   DePalma, R. (2013). Choosing to lose our gender expertise: Queering sex/gender in school settings. *Sex Education: Sexuality, Society and Learning*, 13(1), 1–15.

alienation—this human creative (as Marx would use the term) potential—to grant themselves the incredible power to determine the "normal" way society determines a person's sex. This "normalcy" becomes the doctor's private property, which grants her special status, authority, and privilege in the world. She is now the "sex expert" who tells everyone else how to identify and behave. "Normal" society backs her up.

In Queer Marxist Theology, trans or "non-binary" people are breaking society's chains—they are refusing the doctor's "assignment" and society's demands. They are refusing the pronouns, the dress, the sexuality, and the behaviors of those who would claim "normal." A trans person makes the reality in their head "the truth" of their world as they materialize their thoughts on their body by way of their own will. Queer Theory argues that trans people are divine beings transcending their fallen physical form. Trans people reveal the "truth of Queer Theory" to the rest of society; they serve to "queer" society. A trans person reflects a transcended humanity back on society to demand changes in how people think about sex, gender, sexuality, and the "normal." A new society—new traditions, norms, and values—then reflects a new human image back on Man. Queer Activists believe that if they can repeat this cycle—Man makes society, society makes Man—enough, they will reach the end of History, realizing their full *queer humanity* and become God.

Go back and re-read Karl Marx's definition of communism, quoted earlier in this chapter. You don't have to change much to adopt Marx's definition of communism to match Queer Theory's stated goals and aspirations. If anything, you might add "queer" before "communism" to denote the plagiarism.

IN SUMMARY

Queer Theory is Queer Marxism, which means Queer Theory is

Queer Marxist Theology. Like classical Marxism, Queer Marxism lusts for complete control over society. Whereas Marx thought Man must be returned to his creative and social(ist) nature, Queer Marxism thinks Man must be returned to his *queer nature*. In this view, all human beings must be affirmed and celebrated for living in whatever reality they say they are living in. Nothing is considered normal, and everyone gets to *become* the most narcissistic person they possibly can be.

Queer Communism cannot be accomplished without force because Queer Activists believe people are too stupid to realize that anything deemed "normal" is categorized as such through a pure fabrication of unjust power. By queering and ultimately controlling society and the State, Queer Activists think they can force people to believe the "truth" of Queer Marxism. They believe they can arrest the steering wheel of History and drive us all off the ledge. Under normal circumstances, all of this nonsense would be cause for endless mockery and laughter. Unfortunately, Queer Activists have proved to be remarkably effective. Today, they already have one hand on the wheel, and our kids are in the car.

Chapter 4

THE CRITICAL TURN
IN EDUCATION

To the question: 'How did Queer Theory get into my child's school, and why is it there?', the most accurate answer would be: Critical Marxists captured the American university system decades ago, paving the way for Queer Activists to *queer* education.

To fully comprehend the *queer* education children receive in schools nationwide, we must explore the Marxist takeover of our educational system. The Marxist cult has long known that education is a crucial lever for jumpstarting and maintaining communist revolutions. Lenin knew that the Bolshevik revolutionaries who made him the first head of Soviet Russia would never live long enough to bask in the glory of their yet-to-be-realized communist society. Lenin created Marxist schools to teach children that "the entire purpose of [your] lives is to build a communist society."[64] Chairman Mao Zedong of the People's Republic of China rose back to power after the catastrophe of his "Great Leap

---

64   Lenin, V. (1920). *The tasks of the youth leagues: Speech delivered at the third*

Forward" policies by brainwashing the youth and using them to ignite his Cultural Revolution. Both men knew that a stranglehold on the schools was a precondition for operational success.

Marxists have learned a lot from the likes of Lenin and Mao, and they've been hammering away at the American schoolhouse with their *Critical Theory* for some time now. Paulo Freire would eventually break the foundation, and Queer Theory would capitalize on the situation by recruiting the children left in the rubble. Bear with me and this brief history lesson. This is a *critical* story.

CRITICAL THEORY

Karl Marx believed that his revolutionary theory of History predicted the inevitable collapse of capitalist society and "the mobilization of the working class toward revolutionary consciousness and activity."[65] Marx was wrong, and a crisis emerged in Marxist theory when socialist movements failed to take root in the Western industrial societies as they had in the largely agrarian Russia and China.

Marxists scrambled in the first half of the 20th century, working to develop an updated Marxist theory to explain why the predictions of classical Marxism never came true. These *neo-Marxists* (Cultural, Western, and Critical Marxists) arrived at the idea that culture plays a vital role in suppressing the revolutionary energy required to spark a communist revolution. Western culture, they believed, brainwashes people into thinking that capitalism is good for them.

all-Russia congress of the Russian Young Communist League. Marxists Internet Archive. Retrieved from https://www.marxists.org/archive/lenin/works/1920/oct/02.htm

65 Thompson, M. J. (2017). Introduction: What is critical theory? In M. J. Thompson (Ed.), *The Palgrave Handbook of Critical Theory* (pp. 1–14). Palgrave Macmillan. (p. 3).

For Gramsci, the culture and practices of the dominant powers of any class-based society would necessitate the deployment of particular cultural norms and mindsets that would dull and inhibit critical consciousness, thereby short-circuiting the radical activity of the working class. Culture was therefore made into a particularly important domain of critique since it was there that power and domination could become woven into the consciousness and everyday life of subjects. Gramsci therefore adds to the ideas of Korsch and Lukacs by showing how cultural ideas, practices and norms could work against the class consciousness and political interest and lead individuals to endorse the very kind of social world they ought to oppose.[66] (Thompson, 2017, p. 5)

The neo-Marxists of the first decades of the 20th century believed they could no longer count on the working class in Western societies to "wake up" on their own and answer the communist's revolutionary call. Neo-Marxists believed that tearing apart Western culture was a prerequisite for convincing people that capitalism must go—a prerequisite for convincing people to throw themselves into the meat grinder of communist revolution.

Neo-Marxists created *Critical Theory* to first weaken and then radically transform Western culture. Whereas a traditional theory of society only seeks to understand or explain a given phenomenon, a critical theory seeks to *critique and change* society. According to Max Horkheimer, the Marxist who coined the term, he created the Critical Theory because the emerging neo-Marxists had concluded they could not describe an ideal society on the terms provided by the existing, oppressive society at all, but they could criticize those aspects of the existing society they wished to change. The way he framed it, a critical theory has three components. First, a critical theory must imagine an

---

66   ibid.

ideal moral society liberated from the oppressive structures of the existing society. Second, a critical theory must ruthlessly critique how the society one lives in falls short of this ideal moral vision. Third, a critical theory must require political activism to change the society one lives in until it matches the ideal moral version of society one wishes to have.

The ideal moral society envisioned by Critical Theory is sold as one where all people are free from domination and oppression. That is, it is a *negative imaginary*, one defined in terms of *not being* any of the things Critical Marxists don't like. For Marxists, there is only one type of society that could meet these criteria—a communist society. Accordingly, the criticisms leveled against the current society by Critical Theory are always Marxist critiques whereby the Marxist complains endlessly that things would be better if only they weren't as they are. Because Critical Theory offers only a negative vision, this can only be accomplished if he, the Critical Theorist, in all of his divine wisdom, were in power. Critical Theory's activism is—you get the picture by now— always Marxist activism to move society towards communism. Critical Theory, in other words, is not really a *theory* at all, as you or I might typically define one. Critical Theory is a *playbook* for Marxist political activism. The goal of Critical Theory is to relentlessly criticize a society's institutions and culture, demanding that those institutions give in to Marxist demands. Marxists *practice* Critical Theory to capture institutions and then use those institutions to generate cultural revolution.

The neo-Marxists practicing Critical Theory (Critical Theorists) in the early and middle 20th century believed Western institutions—the media, education, the church, the family, and law—churned out social norms and culture that brainwashed and stabilized the working class, preventing Marx's predicted class consciousness from sparking a communist revolution. So, they set out to capture these institutions with Critical Theory and develop a revolutionary counterculture within them. Neo-Marxists endlessly critiqued the media, education, the church, the family, and the law for all the ways these institutions were falling short of the Marxist vision. They demanded seats at the tables of power so they could turn those institutions into Marxist institutions and use them to feed the working class a revolutionary consciousness they so desperately wanted it to have.

Of course, in most cases, the language these saboteurs used wasn't so blatant. Marxists are well known for redefining words and not telling you about it. For instance, Marxists have historically used the word "justice" very deceptively in their ruthless critiques of society to convince people to support things they otherwise wouldn't. What Marxists don't tell their target audience is that they believe that a "just" society necessarily *limits individual freedoms*, or, as Marx Horkheimer stated in an interview in 1969, "Freedom and justice are dialectical concepts. The more freedom, the less justice and the more justice, the less freedom."[67] In other words, Marxists claim that if people are free to do what they want, then they might, say, support and maintain capitalism. We know how the Marxists feel about that. For them, capitalism breeds inequality, so it must be taken off the table so that no one can choose it. Neo-Marxists infiltrators have long claimed that various American "systems" and institutions are "unjust." What they've always meant is that they think Americans are too free. Marxists know their utopia is only possible when everyone is equally free to shut up, sit down, and enjoy the ride.

As the 20th century progressed, it became increasingly clear that Western citizens were not interested in Marxism. Marxists

67   Murphy, M. (2014, October 3). *'The more justice, the less freedom': Max Horkheimer on Critical Theory*. Social Theory Applied. Retrieved from https://socialtheoryapplied.com/2014/10/03/4204

were disillusioned that their cultural revolution wasn't working out so well in places like America. At the time, many Americans were thoroughly anti-communist and knew the sound of bullshit when they heard it. But Marxists weren't ready to give up on Marxism or America, so they continued working on their Critical Theory, tinkering away and incorporating new ideas about culture and society, hoping to finally crack the revolutionary code.

The Critical Theorist Herbert Marcuse deserves the largest share of credit for figuring out how to sell Critical Theory (Marxism) to an American audience. By the 1960s, Marcuse understood that all the trappings of American life had stabilized the traditional Marxist targets. The working class was happy to go to work, happy to aspire to join the middle class, and happy to watch TV, buy their decent cars, and go on the occasional holiday with their children. Marcuse knew that, if anything, the working class was now a *counter-revolutionary* force. So, he developed a new vector of attack that would target what he called the "militant intelligentsia" and "ghetto populations" instead. Marcuse thought these groups could be radicalized more easily by teaching them how to wield Critical Theory before sending them back into the working class to sow chaos and destabilize it.

Very different from the revolution at previous stages of history, this opposition is directed against the totality of a well-functioning, prosperous society – a protest against its Form – the commodity form of men and things, against the imposition of false values and a false morality. This new consciousness and the instinctual rebellion isolate such opposition from the masses and from the majority of organized labor, the integrated majority, and make for the concentration of radical politics in active minorities, mainly among the young middle-class intelligentsia, and among the ghetto populations. Here, prior to all political strategy and organization, liberation becomes a vital, "biological" need.[68] (Marcuse, 1969)

Marcuse's agenda marked a fundamental change in Marxist strategy. The working class was too big to chew all at once, so Marcuse set out to divide the working class from within. Rather than attempting to radicalize all working-class people by telling them that U.S. economic conditions are fundamentally unfair, Marcuse argued for radicalizing specific subgroups of people that would be more welcoming to the Marxist sales pitch. The strategy was straightforward: first, radicalize college kids who, in their disastrous idealism and absolute ignorance, would then move on to work in the institutions that Marxists wished to infiltrate and capture. From these institutions—like education—the young professional radicals could inspire Marxist cultural changes from the top-down. Second, radicalize disenfranchised pockets of America who can agitate for and demand revolutionary social change from the bottom-up. The goal was to convince "ghetto populations," the unemployed, sexual minorities, feminists, and anyone else who had grievances, to become so enamored with socialism that it would literally become a "biological need" in their lives. That is to say, Marcuse advocated for getting college kids and suffering populations so hooked on Marxism that they would think they couldn't live without it. Meanwhile, writing in *Counterrevolution and Revolt* in 1972 after the radicalism of the late 1960s failed to produce the desired results, he urged his brainwashed acolytes to go into the various professions, including "education at all levels," and take their Critical Marxist theory and praxis in with them.

---

68 Marcuse, H. (1969). *An essay on liberation*. Marxists Internet Archive. https://www.Marxists.org/reference/archive/marcuse/works/1969/essay-liberation.htm

FROM EDUCATION TO CRITICAL EDUCATION

Marcuse's strategy proved highly effective, especially with America's youth, who took their radicalism into the university and eventually made U.S. education *critical*. In *The Critical Turn In Education*, Iowa State University's Marxist educational activist Isaac Gottesman explains:

> "To the question: 'Where did all the sixties radicals go?', the most accurate answer," noted Paul Buhle (1991) in his classic *Marxism in the United States*, "would be: neither to religious cults nor yuppiedom, but to the classroom." (p. 263) After the fall of the New Left arose a new left, an Academic Left. For many of these young scholars, Marxist thought, and particularly what some refer to as Western Marxism or neo-Marxism, and what I will refer to as the critical Marxist tradition, was an intellectual anchor. As participants in the radical politics of the sixties entered graduate school and moved into faculty positions and started publishing, the *critical turn* began to change scholarship throughout the humanities and social sciences. The field of education was no exception.[69] (Gottesman, 2016, p. 1)

The cult of Marcuse rushed into universities in the '60s, '70s, and '80s. The *critical turn* in education saw Marxism take hold of the steering wheel, turning the U.S. university system away from educating college students to succeed in a well-functioning society and towards brainwashing them to practice *Critical Theory* and become revolutionary political agents. The critical turn splintered Critical Theory into *Critical Theories*. That is, the radicals who rushed onto campus during the critical turn took

---

69 Gottesman, I. (2016). *The critical turn in education: From Marxist critique to poststructuralist feminism to critical theories of race* (1st ed.). Routledge.

Critical Theory with them, applying it to specific disciplines to generate new, more targeted Marxist political programs.

For instance, Marxist activists applied Critical Theory to the study of the law, creating Critical Legal Studies (CLS). CLS activists argued that U.S. laws were developed to maintain the status quo of society and codify systemic biases towards marginalized groups. Then, some CLS scholars, upset that the field was "too white," ventured off on their own and applied Critical Theory to the existing scholarship concerned with race and racism, creating Critical Race Theory (CRT). Critical Race Theorists, according to themselves, "question the very foundations of the liberal order, including equality theory, legal reasoning, Enlightenment rationalism, and neutral principles of constitutional law."[70] They argue that white people created a white supremacist society, gave themselves a special form of (Bourgeois) private property called "whiteness," and used the hidden privileges afforded to them by "whiteness" to maintain a racial hierarchy to their economic, political, and cultural benefit. This hierarchy needs to be resisted by awakening a critical race consciousness—also known as "anti-racism." Sounds a lot like Marxism, but with race, doesn't it?[71]

Nowhere was the Left's institutional capture and application of Critical Theory more devastating than in schools of education, where Marcuse's radicals laid the groundwork for the wholesale import of Paulo Freire's *Critical Theory of education.*

[Paulo] Freire...argued that education must *always* be central to the theory and practice of building movements for radical social change because, regardless of context, it is through education

---

70   Delgado, R., & Stefancic, J. (2017). *Critical Race Theory: An Introduction* (3rd ed.). NYU Press. (p. 21).
71   See *Race Marxism: The Truth About Critical Race Theory and Praxis* by James Lindsay.

that consciousness about one's position within the social order is obtained. This is the central feature of his critical educational approach and his unique contribution to Marxist revolutionary theory. Freire's critical work thus became helpful for many in thinking through and passionately articulating how and why schooling, and education more generally, should be harnessed in the push against an (increasingly theorized and understood) unjust social order. As even a cursory glance at literature in the field makes clear, over the past 25 years *Pedagogy of the Oppressed* has become *the* citation for signaling a scholar's belief in education as an emancipatory process within an unjust social order.[72] (Gottesman, 2016, p. 26)

As Gottesman correctly identifies, Paulo Freire is a *titan* in the field of education. The Brazilian Marxist educator's influence on U.S. education cannot be overstated. Freire isn't just a highly cited author for those "scholar[s] beli[eving] in education as an emancipatory process within an unjust social order." He is *the* citation for all of U.S. education. You can't earn your teaching degree in America without being touched by Paulo Freire's Critical Theory and methods. You find his influence in every nook and cranny of U.S. education, from how teachers are trained to design and implement curriculum to how schools now discipline students (Restorative Justice). Most relevant for this book, Freire is *the guy* who makes the act of teaching Queer Theory to children possible. To not know Freire is not to know anything about what's happening in schools today.

Paulo Freire argued that normal educational practices literally "deposit" society—with all of its oppression and "dehumanization" (as Marx would understand it)—into learners. Freire argued that traditional educational methods taught learners to

---

72   Gottesman, I. (2016). *The critical turn in education: From Marxist critique to poststructuralist feminism to critical theories of race* (1st ed.). Routledge.

accept and reproduce the unjust status-quo of society without question. In this sense, traditional curriculum and teaching methods brainwash learners into what Freire called a *magical consciousness* (often called a "false consciousness" in Marxist literature). Someone with a magical consciousness doesn't understand how oppression works, how oppressed they are, or how to answer the Marxist's revolutionary call. Being the Marxist theologian and activist that he was, Freire felt compelled to develop a Marxist theory of education that could reveal the call of revolution to those charged with advancing humanity to the next stage of History.

Freire claimed that the true purpose of education was to help learners cast off their magical consciousness and push them to develop *critical consciousness*. Critical consciousness is the belief that one must "read" sociopolitical conditions *critically* and take action. What this means in layman's terms is that someone who has critical consciousness believes that everything in society is designed to oppress them, and the only way to see "the truth" about the world is to become a Marxist who practices Critical Theories. A person who has developed critical consciousness is *woke* (a *critical constructivist* in Marxist jargon), meaning they have *awakened* to the "prophetic vision" of the postmodern neo-Marxist faith. Freire said the purpose of this consciousness is to denounce the existing world in a critical way so that it announces the possibility of a transformed new world premised on neo-Marxist "liberation."

People who have critical consciousness are religious fanatics hell-bent on breaking society and steering us toward the end of History. This is not hyperbole. Henry Giroux, a close friend of Paulo Freire and one of the most influential educational academics in all of North America, once described Freire's Marxist faith and methods as the "view [that] the kingdom of God [is] something to be created on earth."[73] If that's not clear enough, Giroux has also said:

> The notion of faith that emerges in Freire's work is informed by the memory of the oppressed, the suffering that must not be allowed to continue, and the need to never forget that the prophetic vision is an ongoing process, a vital aspect of the very nature of human life. In short, by combining the discourses of critique and possibility *Freire joins history and theology* [emphasis added] in order to provide the theoretical basis for a radical pedagogy that combines hope, critical reflection, and collective struggle (Giroux, 1985, pp. xvii).[74]

Paulo Freire *applied Critical Theory to education* to break what he considered a ruling class mechanism for maintaining the status quo. He developed a Marxist vision of what education should be—education *for* critical consciousness. In fact, it's specifically and deliberately Maoist, as Freire himself notes. Writing in his magnum opus, *Pedagogy of the Oppressed*, Freire observes from the first chapter,

> The pedagogy of the oppressed, as a humanist and libertarian pedagogy, has two distinct stages. In the first, the oppressed unveil the world of oppression and through the praxis commit themselves to its transformation. In the second stage, in which the reality of oppression has already been transformed, this pedagogy ceases to belong to the oppressed and becomes a pedagogy of all people in the process of permanent liberation. In both stages, it is always

---

73 Giroux, H. (1985). Introduction. In P. Freire, *The Politics of Education: Culture, Power and Liberation*. Bergin & Garvey Publishers. (pp. xvii).
74 ibid.

through action in depth that the culture of domination is culturally confronted. (Freire, p. 54)[75]

This passage contains the following footnote in Freire's book: "This appears to be the fundamental aspect of Mao's Cultural Revolution."[76]

Freire then critiqued traditional educational methods for all of the ways they don't lead to the development of critical consciousness in learners. Finally, he developed teaching methods and practices for achieving his vision. His method is simple: academic material like literacy lessons become "mediators" to political knowledge, which is to say Critical Marxist interpretation. That is, academic material becomes an excuse to talk about radicalizing political issues on Critical Marxist terms. Freire's vision, critique, and method amount to a Marxist theory of education explicitly predicated on the success of Mao Zedong in China that Marxists could practice on learners to brainwash them into the Marxist faith.

At its core, Paulo Freire's Marxist theory of education is a Marxist *theory of knowledge.* Freire calls into question what knowledge is, who defines it, who certifies it, and who determines what knowledge is taught in the classroom. For Freire, only the oppressed have "true" knowledge of their "concrete" conditions, and traditional educational methods only serve to ignore this "true" knowledge while forcing learners to accept "the truth" as society wants them to see it. The oppressed (and children) are already *knowers,* though they don't know what their knowledge, which is their lived experience, means because that has been hidden from them. In the *critical* classroom, no "true"

---

75   Freire, P. (2005). *Pedagogy of the Oppressed* (30th anniversary ed.). Continuum
76   ibid.

knowledge exists outside the "true" knowledge of the Marxist analysis of oppression and the "truth" of Marxism. Thus, Freire's Critical Theory of education is all about privileging the "lived experiences" of students who "know" the "truth" of their "concrete" realities. Broadly speaking:

> critical education seeks to expose how relations of power and inequality (social, cultural, economic) in their myriad of forms, combinations, and complexities, are manifest and are challenged in the formal and informal education of children and adults. In its most robust form, it involves a throughout-going reconstruction of what education is for, how it should be carried out, what we should teach, and who should be empowered to engage in it.[77] (Gottesman, 2016, p. xii)

Freire described his Critical Theory of education as "liberatory" and "humanizing," by which he means teaching people how to liberate all people from oppression and humanize (as Marx would use the term) the world. In his 2000 book *The Pedagogy of Freedom*, he also describes it this way: "the teaching-learning process, together with the work of research, is essential and an inseparable aspect of the gnostic cycle," indicating that it is a process of gnostic cult awakening rather than education. The explicit goal of Freire's methods is to motivate learners to become awakened (or Woke) revolutionary activists charged with denouncing everything and, in so doing, announcing the "prophetic vision" of the communist utopia that follows.

One of the basic questions that we need to look at is how to convert merely rebellious attitudes into revolutionary ones in the process of

---

77   Gottesman, I. (2016). *The critical turn in education: From Marxist critique to poststructuralist feminism to critical theories of race* (1st ed.). Routledge.

the radical transformation of society. Merely rebellious attitudes or actions are insufficient, though they are an indispensable response to legitimate anger. It is necessary to go beyond rebellious attitudes to a more radically critical and revolutionary position, which is in fact a position not simply of denouncing injustice but of announcing a new utopia.[78] (Freire, 1998, p. 54)

Furthermore, Freire sees this process in explicitly religious terms, calling it a process of death and rebirth and even comparing it to a personal Easter. "The *sine qua non* the apprenticeship demands is that, first of all, they really experience their own Easter, that they die as elitists so as to be resurrected on the side of the oppressed, that they be born again with the beings who were not allowed to be."[79] He describes this personal "Easter" in stark, cultic terms explicitly designed to displace Christianity:

This Easter, which results in the changing of consciousness, must be existentially experienced. The real Easter is not commemorative rhetoric. It is praxis; it is historical involvement. The old Easter of rhetoric is dead—with no hope of resurrection. It is only in the authenticity of historical praxis that Easter becomes the death that makes life possible. But the bourgeois world view, basically necrophiliac (death-loving) and therefore static, is unable to accept this supremely biophiliac (life-loving) experience of Easter. The bourgeois mentality—which is far more than just a convenient abstraction—kills the profound historical dynamism of Easter and turns it into no more than a date on the calendar.[80] (*Freire, 1985, p. 123*)

---

78   Freire, P. (1998). *Pedagogy of Freedom: Ethics, Democracy, and Civic Courage.* Rowman & Littlefield Publishers.
79   Freire, P. (1985). *The Politics of Education: Culture, Power and Liberation.* Bergin & Garvey Publishers. (pp. 122-123).
80   ibid.

Freire puts his educational theory (read: cult religion) into practice through *Critical Pedagogy*. We'll discuss Critical Pedagogy at length in *Chapter 6*. For now, it's essential to know that education schools picked up Freire's Critical Theory of education and Critical Pedagogy after the *critical turn* in education, which means they have been pumping out *critical educators* (those who received a *critical* education) for decades. This is not an exaggeration. All education schools in the United States push Freire's Marxist theory of education and pedagogical practices in their programs. Freire's theory dominates our education schools, and critical educators believe that the only way to reduce inequality and achieve "social justice" is to push kids to develop critical consciousness and become political activists.

FROM FREIRE TO CULTURALLY RELEVANT TEACHING

Paulo Freire's theory and methods were introduced to the U.S. in the 1980s, where they spread like wildfire, thanks in large part to the tireless efforts of Henry Giroux. In *The Marxification of Education*, bestselling author and world-renowned anti-Marxist Dr. James Lindsay describes Giroux's "evangelism" and Paulo Freire's reception in North America this way:

> Thanks to the relentless efforts ("praxis") of Critical Marxist educators, most of all his disciple and evangelist Henry Giroux, who is openly a Communist, Freire's work was eventually welcomed into the heart of the North American academic educational canon. This occurred significantly because of the tireless work of Giroux and other Critical Pedagogues in the 1970s and 1980s. Giroux deserves the most blame for this unlikely feat, however, since he personally worked through the first half of the 1980s to see that at least one hundred Critical Marxists were tenured as professors in colleges of

education. Thus, by the time Paulo Freire's 1985 book *The Politics of Education* burst onto the North American scene following a favorable review in the *Harvard Educational Review* in that same year, the Critical Pedagogy runway was laid, and the plane carrying this failure of an educational model could land in the North American education scene. (Lindsay, 2022, p. 8)

Freire was wholly embraced by an Academic Left in education that now enjoyed status and tenure. From their ivory tower, they studied his works with what can only be described as a cult religious conviction. Books like *Pedagogy of the Oppressed*, *The Politics of Education*, and *Education for Critical Consciousness* convinced (read: conned) educators to completely abandon what U.S. education once was (already *heavily* influenced by the Social Reconstructionists) in favor of Freire's "prophetic vision." Education was now more about social engineering than learning, more about addressing inequality than imparting knowledge, and more about *Critical Social Justice* than reading, writing, and math.

Many people picked up Freire's torch, busily trying to figure out how to adopt Freire's theory and methods first to teacher education programs and then to K–12 education. Freire situated his work in the context of poor and illiterate Brazilian farmers, so his methods required tweaking to make more sense in a country where the primary political pain points were race, sex, and sexuality rather than economic class or colonial status. Luckily for the critical educators who would contribute most to the project of situating Freire's theory into a U.S. context—Henry Giroux, Peter McLaren, Joe Kincheloe, and Gloria Ladson-Billings—the university system was already bursting at the seams with new Critical Theories of race, ethnicity, culture, sex, and sexuality.

The pioneers of North American Critical Pedagogy (Marxist

teaching methods) drew from postcolonial theory, critical multiculturalism, postmodernism, Critical Race Theory, and Queer Theory. They made Critical Pedagogy interdisciplinary to incorporate the elements needed to address specific domains of oppression. For instance, if an educator was working with black children they could employ a *Critical Race Pedagogy* (Critical Race Theory + Critical Pedagogy) to help those children develop their *critical race consciousness*. Or, if an educator was addressing the topics of sex, gender, and sexuality, they could employ *Queer Pedagogy* (Queer Theory + Critical Pedagogy) to help those children develop their *queer consciousness*.

Although you can find numerous examples of grade school teachers deploying Critical Pedagogy in their classrooms as early as the 1980s, it wasn't until Gloria Ladson-Billings developed "Culturally Relevant Teaching" that Critical Pedagogy went mainstream in children's classrooms. Ladson-Billings, the Marxist educator who popularized Culturally Relevant Teaching (the other "CRT"), is one of Freire's direct theoretical descendants. Several generations removed from Freire's canonical texts, many of today's teachers and administrators have no idea that Freire's Critical Theory of education underpins one of their most prized educational concepts.

Paulo Freire considered economic class, reinforced through colonial occupation, the primary axis of oppression, meaning he thought that the Bourgeoisie used traditional education to stratify society between a ruling class and a working class or peasants. Ladson-Billings was educated during the critical turn in education when Marxists mostly abandoned the working class while busily applying Critical Theory to identity politics. Her education left her convinced that teachers could only be successful in "liberating" their students if they were equipped with unique theories and tools to address not only class but race, ethnicity, sexuality, and culture in their classrooms. Following this conviction and drawing on the works of other Marxist education scholars like Michael Apple, Peter McLaren, Henry Giroux, and Elizabeth Ellsworth, Ladson-Billings took Freire's Maoist framework and customized it for U.S. schools. She developed her theory of Culturally Relevant Teaching to address multiple domains of oppression, not just economic class. Culturally Relevant Teaching, in other words, is *intersectional* (specifically, it is Intersectional Maoism, which James Lindsay calls "Maoism with American Characteristics"). It is meant to address the cumulative way in which multiple forms of discrimination combine, overlap, and intersect in the lives and experiences of students.[81]

Like the *Freirean* teacher, the culturally relevant teacher's job is explicitly given as to develop a critical consciousness in students, teaching them how to use a Marxist sociopolitical analysis to understand how their cultural identity (race, sex, "gender," etc.) and "lived experiences" are excluded from classrooms and society. In practice, this means telling children that a ruling class (dominant culture) oppresses them because they are poor, black, Hispanic, Native American, a girl, gay, lesbian, "trans," or fat. After learning that they are oppressed, children are meant to begin practicing *critical reflection*—reflecting on their culture, identity, and experiences from a Marxist standpoint. This critical reflection is designed to motivate students to take up radical political activism, just as Freire prescribed. Gloria Ladson-Billings was explicit about her program's goals when she published *Toward A Theory of Culturally Relevant Pedagogy* in 1995. "Culturally relevant teaching must," she observes, "[lead to

---

81   Merriam-Webster. (n.d.). *Intersectionality.* In Merriam-Webster.com dictionary. Retrieved from https://www.merriam-webster.com/dictionary/intersectionality

the] development of a sociopolitical or critical consciousness."[82] Furthermore, she writes:

> Beyond individual characteristics of academic achievement and cultural competence, students must develop a broader sociopolitical consciousness that allows them to critique the cultural norms, values, mores, and institutions that produce and maintain social inequalities.[83] (Ladson-Billings, 1995)

School administrators and teachers today have been trained to believe that Culturally Relevant Teaching is the only way to ensure their instructional methods are "diverse, equitable, and inclusive." Ladson-Billings, in fact, described her Freirean approach in 1995 with the tagline, "But that's just good teaching." Culturally Relevant Teaching is now considered an essential practice for eliminating achievement gaps between student groups, reducing classroom conflict, and maximizing every student's "equal shot at the same outcome (read: equity)," as it is so often phrased. Today, teachers everywhere are trained to think they must make their materials and methods "culturally relevant" for children to be successful in school. Most of these teachers have been duped, but many *know* what they are doing.

At its core, Culturally Relevant Teaching forwards the idea that many children fail in school because there is a cultural mismatch between their school and their home/community. Culturally Relevant Teachers assume that "academic knowledge and skills" must be situated "within students' lived experiences and frames of reference"[84] to be learned. Therefore, students

---

82 Ladson-Billings, G. (1995). Toward a theory of culturally relevant pedagogy. *American Educational Research Journal*, 32(3), 465–491.
83 ibid.
84 Gay, G. (2002). Preparing for culturally responsive teaching. *Journal of Teacher Education*, 53(2), 106–116.

who can learn, read, write, talk, and behave at school like they do at home or in their community—a cultural match between school and student—are more likely to succeed. Students who are removed from their cultural reference points and "lived experiences" at school face a cultural mismatch, making them less likely to succeed. Put simply, Culturally Relevant Teachers believe that schools privilege some cultures while "silencing" and excluding others.

Culturally Relevant Teachers argue that schools hide the harmful effects of cultural mismatch in a "myth of meritocracy" that blinds teachers and students to the pernicious dynamic at play. As Gloria Ladson-Billings notes in *Toward A Theory of Culturally Relevant Pedagogy*, "the goal of education becomes how to 'fit' students...into [a] hierarchical structure that is defined as *meritocracy*."[85] Culturally Relevant Teachers think that schools are not and have never been meritocratic. They think that "success" in school has always reflected how well a student assimilates into the dominant culture(s).

Culturally Relevant Teaching rests on the idea that schools stabilize the oppressive social and economic order by only accepting "normal" ways of reading, writing, thinking, and behaving. That is, Culturally Relevant Teaching rests on the idea that schools only accept certain forms of *knowledge* and certain people as *knowers*. In this view, the dominant culture in society has defined what counts as the normal way to read, write, and behave, and it measures all students' success against those unjust benchmarks. Like Paulo Freire, Culturally Relevant Teachers argue that a dominant culture uses schools to stratify society, creating a hierarchy where the most "educated" (normal) reign supreme.

In summary, Culturally Relevant Teaching claims that the

---

85 Ladson-Billings, G. (1995). Toward a theory of culturally relevant pedagogy. *American Educational Research Journal*, 32(3), 465–491.

dominant culture uses schools to sustain and reproduce itself. The goal of the Culturally Relevant Teacher is to tailor her methods and practices to identify and deconstruct this dominant culture. She must determine how the dominant culture(s) marginalizes other cultures—other ways of reading, writing, doing math, practicing science, behaving, and "knowing the truth"—in her classroom. Likewise, the goal of the Culturally Relevant Teacher is to help students deconstruct their own culture(s) and determine how they specifically are oppressed by the dominant culture(s), or how their culture(s) oppress the marginalized culture(s). After modeling this deconstruction, the Culturally Relevant Teacher's mission is to empower and inspire her students to change the dominant culture through social justice activism. Her job is to push her students to develop critical consciousness.

FROM CULTURALLY RELEVANT TEACHING TO QUEER EDUCATION

Like Freire's original works, Culturally Relevant Teaching practices spread like wildfire in the *critical* American academy. Marxists had already worked for three decades to undermine American education by the time Ladson-Billings's *Towards a Theory of Culturally Relevant Pedagogy* hit anyone's radar in the late 1990s. The establishment was already convinced that traditional educational methods were inherently unjust and must be completely overhauled. Culturally Relevant Teaching was easy to sell to a ravenous mob that was under incredible pressure to leave *no child behind.*

As Critical Pedagogy(s) like Culturally Relevant Teaching spread, so did Queer Theory. Queer Theory bubbled out of the academy at the same time as Culturally Relevant Teaching, and it was embraced with a similar passion. Critical educators were hooked on Freire's "prophetic vision" of education, and they mixed and matched new Critical Theories as fast as they popped up. America is a complex melting pot, and every aspect of student identity—race, class, sex, or sexuality—needed to be accounted for in the increasingly *intersectional* witch's brew. Queer Theory was the perfect complement to a Culturally Relevant Teaching with much to say about race but too little to say about sex, gender, and sexuality. Said another way, culturally relevant teachers needed somewhere to turn to figure out how to handle the culture of sex, gender, and sexuality in the American classroom. Queer Theory answered the call as the bodies of *Women's Studies* and *Gay and Lesbian Studies* lay unconscious on the floor.

Queer Theory was built to run on the machine that is Freire's Marxist theory of education. In a sense, Freire's ideas had already queered U.S. education prior to Queer Theory's ascent in the academy. Freire's theory of education is one that challenges existing concepts of knowledge and who counts as a knower. In fact, the heart of Freire's argument, which finds its home in all of education today, is that learners must be taught how to dismantle the "mythical norms" of society. Queer Theory is entirely concerned with analyzing and *abolishing norms*, so educators who shared Freire's faith found Queer Theory to be a potent tool that they could incorporate into their teaching practices.

The generation of activist researchers, teacher-educators, and teachers that followed in the footsteps of Freire, Gloria Ladson-Billings, and others pushed Queer Theory into schools so they could challenge the status-quo of cultural norms related to sex, gender, and sexuality. Activists like bell hooks pushed the intersectional aspects of race, sex, and gender into education through books like *Teaching to Transgress*, and, according to Isaac Gottesman, the poststructuralist feminists, who were precursors to Queer Theorists, made headway at bringing their ideas into the classroom on the back of the critical turn. These activists and others more directly located in Critical Pedagogy believed that "every dimension of schooling and every form of education practice are politically contested spaces"[86] that must be fought for. So, drawing on their *critical* roots, they set out to radically politicize their classrooms as they developed their "social activist teacher persona[s]."[87]

No stone would be left unturned in the schoolhouse. Queer Activists began queering not just the school curriculum but school policies and procedures, all under the guise of becoming more "culturally relevant," "diverse," "equitable," and "inclusive." Each advance was accompanied by the moral weight of an argument to increase "LGBT empathy," "visibility," and "representation." To be abundantly clear, many of these Queer Activists had no idea that they were, in fact, Queer Activists. They thought they were simply embracing the latest and best educational practices to improve schooling, especially for kids who might have a tougher time. Most of the educators who have irrevocably harmed education—and therefore children—over the past three decades aren't aware that their theory of education and teaching practices are derived from the works of Paulo Freire, Michel Foucault, Henry Giroux, Herbert Gintis, Samuel Bowles, Joe Kincheloe, Peter McLaren, Gloria-Ladson Billings, Geneva Gay, Mary K. Bryson, Suzanne de Castell, Jack Halberstam, Deborah Britzman, Judith Butler and many *others*. Still, despite their ignorance, the literature is unambiguous. Educators today have inherited a *critical* orientation towards schooling from these revolutionary radicals, who have been explicit about their intentions and goals for a very long time.

---

86   Kincheloe, J. L. (2008). *Critical Pedagogy primer*. Peter Lang (p. 2).
87   ibid.

it is imperative that we ask how teachers can affirm the voices of marginalized students, engage them *critically* [emphasis added], while at the same time assist them in transforming their communities into sites of struggle and resistance. For critical educators this means that within the context of the larger society, schools must be reconceived as sites of cultural disjuncture, as convulsions within the operating logic of capitalism, and as counter-hegemonic spheres which generate unprecedented possibilities for social critique and utopian thinking.[88] (McLaren & Hammer, 1989, p. 41)

Our children all now attend "culturally relevant," "diverse," "equitable," "sustainable," and "inclusive" schools, which means they are all attending schools that push them to develop critical consciousness. Queer Marxism is practiced in nearly every school in America today because Marxists captured U.S. education decades ago. In effect, Freire's Critical Theory of education queered U.S. education—his theory, carried into classrooms by an army of cult religious followers, transformed the typical education we expect our children to receive into *critical education*. Freire spearheaded a *religious revival* that claimed the true purpose of education is education *for* "social justice," which is education that "recognizes inequality as deeply embedded in the fabric of society (i.e., as structural), and actively seeks to change this."[89]

The leaders and educators who roll off the critical education assembly lines in colleges of education across the country believe they have a moral responsibility to push kids into critical consciousness. Take, for example, this summary of

---

88   McLaren, P., & Hammer, R. (1989). Critical pedagogy and the postmodern challenge: Towards a critical postmodernist pedagogy of liberation. *Educational Foundations*, 3(3): 29–62.
89   Sensoy, Ö., & DiAngelo, R. J. (2017). *Is everyone really equal?: An introduction to key concepts in social justice education*. Teachers College Press. (p. 20).

"culturally responsive" school leadership found in the popular book *Leadership for Increasingly Diverse Schools*:

> Because minoritized students have been disadvantaged by historically oppressive structures, and because educators and schools have been—intentionally or unintentionally—complicit in reproducing this oppression, culturally responsive school leaders have a principled, moral responsibility to counter this oppression.[90] (Scanlan & Theoharis, 2020, p. 1)

The people running our schools today think that they must make schools "diverse," "equitable," and "inclusive" to counter the omnipresent forces of racism, sexism, genderism, and transphobia that are said to be lurking in traditional assessments and classroom practices. Our school leaders and teachers think that some students achieve more than others because the normal way children have been educated for decades is unfair and oppressive. While this means that teachers practice many variations of Critical Pedagogy on children, Queer Theory is the most destructive—*by far*.

Critical education aims to "help students understand reality more critically *and* lay a foundation for students to become the activist changemakers and leaders of mass movements of the present and future."[91] Queer Theory achieves this goal and more, pushing children into the Queer Cult and convincing them that they must not only transform society but they must also do so by transforming themselves. Parents must understand how Queer Theory is practiced in schools if they wish to protect their

---

90   Theoharis, G., & Scanlan, M. (Eds.). (2020). *Leadership for increasingly diverse schools* (2nd ed.). Routledge.
91   Au, W. (2018). *A Marxist education: Learning to change the world*. Haymarket Books. (p. 51).

children from the Marxist groomers who attempt to recruit them for revolution by poisoning their minds and bodies. Parents must know what a *queer* classroom looks like, how the brainwashing lessons in these queer classrooms actually work, and how Queer Activists will do everything in their power to subvert parental authority and hide the queering of their children. We've studied the cult's origins and theory. We now know what Queer Theory is, where it comes from, and how it got into schools. It's now time to study how Queer Theory is *practiced*.

PART 2: PRACTICE

PART THREE

Chapter 5

THE QUEER
CLASSROOM

Queer Activists create queer classrooms, and queer classrooms are all about *inclusion*. The Queer Theory literature describes inclusion as a journey without a destination, a range of "possibilities" without closure. When Queer Activists say a space is "inclusive," they aren't describing a static state, normally interpreted to mean, "everyone here is included, respected, and valued." Inclusion, like the practice of queering, is a never-ending practice. A space can only ever be in the state of "becoming inclusive" through constant denunciation, interrogation, and transformation. It *becomes* inclusive through endlessly excluding anything that Queer Activists want removed.

Inclusion first entered the educational lexicon in the context of student disability. In this context, inclusion meant valuing students with disabilities as active participants in schooling, deserving of the support needed to "succeed in the academic, social, and extra-curricular activities" of schools.[92] Queer Activists have since *queered inclusion*. Today, "inclusion" is the practice of radically politicizing an environment on Queer Theory's terms, forcing anything that might make someone feel "unsafe" or "unwelcome" out the door. The practice of inclusion requires a Marxist socio-political analysis to determine who is marginalized and oppressed and what "safety" and "feeling included" look like for those groups.

In practice, "inclusion" is more precisely defined as "a lack of exclusion," where exclusion is caused by the presence of the evil spirits Queer Theory names, like cisheteronormativity. Queer Activists believe they have the correct knowledge about the way the world works. They think that only through their insight, theory, and practice can "exclusion" be identified and rooted out so all students can feel safe and included. Everyone else is, in their view, too stupid to see and understand oppression.

By accepting this definition of inclusion—as a lack of exclusion—school administrators and educators open themselves up to be completely colonized, captured, and controlled by Queer Theory. Bad news, bears—they have.

CONQUERING LANGUAGE

Inclusive classrooms are classrooms where everyone must be made to feel like they are included by excluding everything Queer Theory doesn't like and compelling everything it does like. From Queer Theory's perspective, it's impossible for all students to feel included in a classroom when heteronormativity (and "normalcy," more broadly) is present. Queer Activists believe that heteronormativity works primarily through language, so they

---

92 McLeskey, J., Spooner, F., Algozzine, B., & Waldron, N. L. (Eds.). (2022). *Handbook of effective inclusive elementary schools: Research and practice* (2nd ed.). Routledge.

are determined to control, compel, and police speech. Queer Activists "think deliberately about language choice" because "the language we use often reflects institutional oppression."[93] To be an "inclusive" educator means eliminating certain words, phrases, and categorizations from the classroom while compelling everyone to speak how Queer Theory wants them to speak.

One of the primary objectives of Queer Activists is to remove "gendered language" from classrooms. Captured school districts like Montgomery County Public Schools (MCPS) in Maryland "center" (read: privilege) LGBTQ+ experiences and voices by denouncing the use of gendered language whenever possible. According to an MCPS staff resource called the *Gender Inclusive Schools Toolkit*, educators should "use language that challenges binary messages about gender and 'de-genders' objects." For example, the resource says that "rather than 'boys and girls,' 'ladies and gentlemen,' etc., refer to pupils as 'students,' 'children,' 'y'all,' 'folks,' your school's mascot (i.e., 'Cougars') or another non-gendered term for the group."[94] Additionally, MCPS's *Guidelines for Student Gender Identity* states that "all students have the right to be referred to by their identified name and/or pronoun. School staff members should address students by the name and pronoun corresponding to the gender identity that is consistently asserted at school."[95]

In creating classroom policies that police the speech of educators, MCPS isn't just eliminating language that Queer Theory seeks to abolish. MCPS is compelling speech, which is an activist

93 Burnes, T. R., & Stanley, J. L. (Eds.). (2017). *Teaching LGBTQ psychology: Queering innovative pedagogy and practice.* American Psychological Association. (p. 45).

94 Gender Spectrum. (n.d.). *Gender inclusive schools toolkit.* Retrieved from https://www.genderspectrum.org

95 Montgomery County Public Schools. (2022–2023). Guidelines for Student Gender Identity. www.montgomeryschoolsmd.org

tactic Queer Activists use to control situations. MCPS doesn't just tell educators that there is some speech they shouldn't use anymore—like calling boys "boys." MCPS tells educators that there is some speech that they must use, like using a student's preferred pronouns. Thus, inclusive policies—like MCPS's gender-neutral language policies—become weapons to justify censorship and purges. It's not just that Queer Activists identify certain words as off-limits—it's that Queer Activists require your tongue to move how they want it to move.

If a school administrator, teacher, or student doesn't agree with Queer Theory, being labeled a bigot is the least of their worries. Many school districts clearly state that Queer Theory is now a legally protected ideology (religion). If you don't use a student's preferred pronouns, you're not only an immoral animal—you're possibly violating nondiscrimination law.

> Montgomery County Public Schools (MCPS) is committed to providing all students with opportunities to succeed and thrive. Part of that commitment is making sure our students have a safe, welcoming school environment where students are engaged in learning and are active participants in the school community because they feel accepted and valued, free from discrimination, bullying, harassment, or intimidation. The Montgomery County Board of Education's core values, guidance from the Maryland State Department of Education, and Montgomery County Board of Education Policy ACA, Nondiscrimination, Equity, and Cultural Proficiency, prohibit discrimination, stigmatization, and bullying based on gender identity, as well as sex, gender, gender expression, and sexual orientation, among other personal characteristics.[96]

Any language that violates Queer Theory's designated parameters

---

96   ibid.

will be considered discriminatory, stigmatizing, and exclusionary. Once Queer Theory enters policy and classroom practice, it becomes incredibly difficult to weed it out. Any suggestion that Queer Theory might not be the best inclusion framework to adopt (I can't think of a worse possible way to do inclusion) might be met with, at best, ostracization and, at worst, legal ramifications. School districts like Wisconsin's Madison Metropolitan School District (MMSD) are explicit about this:

> Having one's gender identity recognized and validated is important. All MMSD staff will refer to students by their affirmed names and pronouns…Refusal to respect a student's name and pronouns is a violation of the MMSD Non-discrimination policy.[97]

Queer Theory bulldozes its way into classrooms under threat of labeling people bigots and conservatives. But, even if a school has managed to keep Queer Theory mostly out by refusing this framing and jamming the bulldozer's tracks, that school must follow the dictates of their State's department of education. Every state has a governing body that oversees the administration of public education, and Queer Theory has captured all of them. For instance, New York City's Department of Education requires that all New York City public school teachers adhere to queered language policies in their classrooms.

> Every student is entitled to be addressed by the name and pronoun that correspond to the student's gender identity that they assert at school…The principal or their designee, in consultation with the

---

97 Madison Metropolitan School District. (2018). *Guidance & Policies to Support Transgender, Non-binary & Gender-Expansive Students*. Retrieved from https://resources.finalsite.net/images/v1625663725/madisonk12wius/m5x6tox6rh rufthykn30/guidancebooklet.pdf

student, is responsible for ensuring that teachers and other school staff are aware of and honor a student's request to be referred to by the name and pronoun that correspond to their gender identity. It is important to note that some students may use gender-neutral pronouns such as they, ze, or other pronouns...All school staff members and students must refer to students by their chosen names and pronouns and schools should create opportunities to confirm the correct information with all their students in a manner that respects student privacy. Intentionally referring to a student, verbally or in writing, by a pronoun inconsistent with the student's gender identity or by a name other than the student's chosen name is unacceptable conduct and may constitute a violation of Chancellor's Regulation A-832, A-830, or A-421.[98]

As we discussed in *Chapter 1*, the U.S. Department of Education itself is wholly captured by Queer Theory. Like all other captured institutions, it hides this under the banner of "welcoming and inclusive" language. And, like all other captured institutions, the U.S. Department of Education is explicit about protecting Queer Theory by folding it into law. Our entire educational infrastructure has been captured and repurposed to queer America's classrooms. Queer Activists, thus far, have won the war of language.

SETTING THE STAGE

Queer Theory can't tolerate silence. Queer Activists think that "silence" literally equates to "violence," which is why they never shut up with that stupid slogan. The logic looks like this—if a person chooses to remain silent about oppression that they're aware of, then that person is consciously deciding to do nothing

---

98 New York City Department of Education. (n.d.). *Guidelines on gender*. Retrieved from https://www.schools.nyc.gov/school-life/school-environment/guidelines-on-gender

about the situation while others suffer. A silent person is, therefore, complicit in that oppression because they are—in effect—saying, "I know this is wrong, but it isn't a big deal for me personally, so I don't care." This profound and brilliant reasoning is why Queer Activists never stop talking, but it's also why they can't resist filling empty space with physical manifestations of their commitment to abolish normalcy.

Visual representations of Queer Theory's ideology serve as a constant reminder that oppression exists, as defined on Queer Theory's terms. On the surface, pride flags are meant to mark a "safe space" for children living in a dangerous world. But when Queer Activists hang pride flags in their classrooms, they aren't *really* trying to send a positive message about the "safety" of their classroom to closeted gay or lesbian kids. They might say that that is what they are doing, but that's only because they haven't stopped to think about the insanity of their worldview for more than five seconds.

In reality, pride flags in classrooms serve as a warning sign, telling all children that the *school outside the classroom* especially, and even the *classroom itself, isn't safe* without Queer Activism. The message is *only places hanging the pride flag have a chance of being safe.* Everywhere else, including the rest of the school, community, and home, is dragged into question. If these spaces were safe, there wouldn't be a need to hang a pride flag in the classroom as a symbol of potential safety. The hanging of a pride flag in a classroom only signals that power dynamics are present, power dynamics which structure social relationships in a way that privileges some students while excluding others. The teacher might be a Queer Activist, but that doesn't mean that a child's classmates are, and it certainly doesn't mean that the teacher across the hall who hangs an American flag on his wall is either. The pride flag hanging on a classroom wall means "danger." The only reason a child needs to see the pride flag, from the Queer Activist's perspective, is to be reminded that schooling "isn't for them" because they don't plug neatly into the normative ideologies—like heteronormativity—they are drowning in. The flag can't make the classroom "safe" unless the structures and systems necessitating its existence are disrupted and dismantled (queered) entirely. And, because classrooms are structured by schools, which are structured by society, all of society must be queered before any classroom can truly be considered safe. They really do believe this.

Queer Activists don't stop at flags, either. Pictures, posters, blankets, murals, banners, and lights all break the awkward and violent silence of a Queer Activist stopping to take a breather. In decorating their classrooms, Queer Activists are bringing Queer Theory to life. Queering the classroom literally sets the stage for teachers and children to begin *performing* sex, gender, and sexuality differently. In queered classrooms, children are encouraged to take to this stage and act silly, "switch genders," play with toys they typically wouldn't associate with, and act *out* everything they've been "programmed" to believe. Children in queer classrooms act out the idea that sex or gender mean anything at all, they act out their physical body, and they act out of heteronormativity.

Sometimes, Queer Activists invite others to join children on the stage. Drag Queen Story Hour (DQSH) is a hot commodity, and Queer Activists nationwide invite drag queen performers into their schools. In 2019, a middle school in Durham, North Carolina, invited local drag queens to perform for children under the guise of "inclusion." Speaking to CNN about the event, the organizers made their motte and bailey clear:

Our drive was to remove barriers to success, belonging and the ability to thrive for all students. It called for a hard look at the roots of these behaviors and intentional actions to liberate not just the bullied from oppressive acts, but the bully from the oppressive root causes of their actions.[99]

Borrowing the terminology of the philosopher Nicholas Schakel, the *motte and bailey* is a rhetorical strategy where a dishonest person switches between two meanings of a word or concept. The "motte" is a highly defensible, non-controversial proposition while the "bailey" is a radical proposition. The dishonest person pushes the bailey until caught, in which case he retreats to the motte position. It's easy to defend "including everyone" and very hard to defend something like Queer Cult grooming. By hiding in the "motte" of "inclusion," Queer Activists like these can lie about and cover up the true intentions of their activities.

In February of 2023, a high school principal in Madison, Wisconsin, used his school's newsletter to promote a "family friendly" drag show "intended to celebrate, affirm, and support…students and staff in our LGBTQIA+ as well as our larger school community."[100] Roughly two hundred students, parents, and staff attended the event. Just a month prior, public schools in Columbia, Missouri, bussed children to a drag queen event without notifying the children's parents that drag queens would be performing.[101] In 2022, it was reported that New York City had

99   CNN. (2019, May 17). *Drag queens recruited to help with pride event.* Retrieved from https://www.cnn.com/2019/05/17/us/drag-queens-recruited-to-help-with-pride-event-trnd/index.html

100   Capital Times. (2023, January 6). *Student-planned drag show at Madison East draws right-wing outrage.* Retrieved from https://captimes.com/news/education/student-planned-drag-show-at-madison-east-draws-right-wing-outrage/article_78c6b2d4-35e9-5e57-b3ef-ac49de7b53ed.html

101   Newsweek. (2023, January 25). *Public school district took middle schoolers to*

spent over two hundred thousand dollars of taxpayer funds on drag events for kids. Drag Story Hour NYC, the nonprofit that NYC's Department of Education couldn't stop throwing money at, organized forty-nine drag programs in thirty-four public elementary, middle, and high schools in just the first six months of that year.

Queer Activists say that bringing drag queens into schools and classrooms is a way to create an inclusive atmosphere for all children. This motte has run roughshod over our schools. To understand the bailey, we turn to *Drag pedagogy: The playful practice of queer imagination in early childhood*. This paper, published in the *Journal of Curriculum Inquiry* in 2021, explains why Queer Activists have suddenly poured a ton of energy into recruiting drag queens to perform for children in schools nationwide.

Drag Queen Story Hour is the program schools buy into when they invite drag queens into their classrooms, libraries, and community events. DQSH is, as the name implies, a story hour where drag queens read books to children while providing a "generative extension of queer pedagogy into the world of early childhood education."[102] Queer Activists explicitly market DQSH as a means of fostering inclusion and empathy in schools and communities. But, as the authors of *Drag pedagogy* make clear, this marketing "is strategically done in order to justify its educational value."

> Though DQSH publicly positions its impact in "help[ing] children
> develop empathy, learn about gender diversity and difference, and

---

drag show without telling their parents. Retrieved from https://www.newsweek.com/public-school-district-took-middle-schoolers-drag-show-without-telling-their-parents-opinion-1776503

102   Keenan, H., & Miss Hot Mess, L. (2021). Drag pedagogy: The playful practice of queer imagination in early childhood. *Childhood Education*, 97(4), 440–461.

tap into their own creativity," we argue that its contributions can run deeper than morals and role models... It is undeniable that DQSH participates in many of these tropes of empathy, from the marketing language the programme uses to its selection of books. Much of this is strategically done in order to justify its educational value.[103]

The goal of inviting kids to a DQSH event isn't to teach them to respect diversity and care for others who may be different than they are. The goal is to use shock and awe to confuse children and, as the authors of *Drag Pedagogy* explicitly state, "bring queer ways of knowing and being into the education of young children."[104] That is to say, the goal is to push drag queens onto children as a "preparatory introduction to *alternate modes of kinship* [emphasis added]." The goal is to induct them into the cult of Queer Theory.

We believe that DQSH offers an invitation towards deeper public engagement with queer cultural production, particularly for young children and their families. It may be that DQSH is "family friendly," in the sense that it is accessible and inviting to families with children, but it is less a sanitizing force than it is a preparatory introduction to alternate modes of kinship. Here, DQSH is "family friendly" in the sense of "family" as an old-school queer code to identify and connect with other queers on the street.[105]

The central learning objective of DQSH is to brainwash kids to believe that "we're all born naked" and "the rest is drag,"[106] directly channeling the Queer Theory of Judith Butler. By stating

103   ibid.
104   ibid.
105   ibid.
106   ibid.

this so clearly, the authors of *Drag Pedagogy* tell us that DQSH serves as an induction ceremony into the cult of Queer Theory. The authors couldn't make this point more explicit even if they read *Gender Trouble* to children during DQSH. The point is to convince kids that "male" and "female," "boy" and "girl" are empty categories that can be filled with anything a child wants to fill them with. The drag queen is the physical embodiment of this learning objective. The person reading books might look like a man but dresses like a woman. His physical appearance "mock[s] authority and challenge[s] the status quo,"[107] and the point of his physical appearance is to teach kids that they too should and can do the same. The performer's presence is a "pathway into the imaginative, messy, and rule-breaking"[108] world of Queer Activism.

DQSH latches onto a child's desire to play and imagine. Learning how to read can be frustrating, tedious, and difficult—but DQSH reading is "dialled [*sic*] up, made more interesting in large part because it is extraordinary."[109]

In the world of drag, you can wear a crown *and* glitter *and* bright yellow crinoline *and* makeup *and* neon green fishnets *and* a wig. Everything is dialled up, made more interesting in large part because it is *extraordinary*. The same book read by a "regular" teacher suddenly seems banal – when a drag queen reads a story, the technicolor has been turned on and the show has begun…The traditional role of the teacher, transformed into a loud and sparkling queen, becomes delightfully excessive. She is less interested in focus, discipline, achievement, or objectives than playful self-expression.

---

107   ibid.
108   ibid.
109   ibid.

Her pedagogy is rooted in pleasure and creativity borne, in part, from letting go of control.[110]

The only thing children learn how to read in DQSH is oppression. The program is designed to make children think gender and sex are social constructs that must be mocked and broken. DQSH is a grooming program for Queer Theory. I don't mean "grooming" as sexual grooming, although there have been many cases of drag queens leading DQSH events who were later found to be *prostitutes and pedophiles*. I mean "grooming" in the sense of "socio-political" or "cult" grooming. DQSH hypes up the color and fun to lull children and adults into a false sense of security, believing something like, "We're just having a lot of fun while learning to read, practicing empathy, and being inclusive." What's actually happening in DQSH is evil for many reasons, perhaps most of which is that it is not an "act of affirmation" of identity at all—it is a "world dismantling effort"[111] that is meant to change children permanently:

> Playing with drag can be a way to remember that, in the words of Harney and Moten, "We're already here, moving" (p. 19). We're dressing up, we're shaking our hips, and we're finding our light – even in the fluorescents. We're reading books while we read each other's looks, and *we're leaving a trail of glitter that won't ever come out of the carpet* [emphasis added].[112]

In fact, their words, "a preparatory introduction to alternate modes of kinship" clearly indicate that Drag Queen Story Hour,

---

110 ibid.
111 ibid.
112 ibid.

like much of the "generative" material in Queer Pedagogy, should be thought of as an *initiation* into the cult of Queer Activism.

NAVIGATING PARENTAL RESISTANCE

Parents in America expect to be the sole determiners of their children's upbringing. *Queer Activists* would like to change that. It's normal for a parent to think they are in charge of raising their child how they want them to be raised. It's more than normal—it's law. In *Washington v. Glucksberg*, the U.S. Supreme Court ruled that the Fourteenth Amendment protects the fundamental right of parents to direct the care, upbringing, and education of their children. But we know the story by now—Queer Activists see normalcy and limitation, and their eyes go red.

Most parents would take issue with the operational deployment of "inclusion" in schools. If the bailey were uncovered, parents everywhere would immediately put an end to the queer education their children are receiving. But parents can mostly not be blamed for what's happened to their schools because Queer Activists are very good at deception. They are so good that there's even a name for their strategy to gaslight and manipulate anyone who might develop concern: navigating parental resistance.

Navigating Parental Resistance: Learning from Responses of LGBTQ-Inclusive Elementary School Teachers can be considered a blueprint for using language to hide Queer Theory instruction from parents. The paper details the rhetorical maneuvers two elementary teachers (one that "identifies as a lesbian and is gender-queer," and another that "identifies as a cisgender, straight ally") use to bulldoze parental concerns and politicize 4th and 5th-grade classrooms filled with nine- and ten-year-olds.

The paper begins by confirming something parents have felt for a while now. Queer Activists think parents are a "significant gatekeeping mechanism" meant to "protect a mythical innocence" that people "project onto children."[113] Queer Theory informs this radical position, which argues that childhood innocence is a "social construct" (go figure!) and parents are foundational in reinforcing and perpetuating "heteronormativity" through the raising of their children. Queer Activists think parents are too stupid and dangerous to be trusted with raising their children to be "inclusive." Therefore, the argument goes, teachers must be deceptive in their method to ensure parents don't get in the way of all the radicalization that must be done. To "challenge the heteronormativity of elementary schools," Queer Activists must be well-versed in navigating parental resistance:

> To Fern and Linda, parents who resisted LGBTQ-inclusive teaching represent status quo power relations that deny equality to those deemed outside of typically represented identities. In their interactions with resistant parents, Linda and Fern lay bare this notion through their language, choices, and expectations, even as they accounted for ways that parents in their community understood power and the place of power in the classroom.[114] (Hermann-Wilmarth & Ryan, 2019, p. 91)

According to the authors, the first place to counter parental resistance is in curriculum planning. This includes couching radical lessons into larger units to forward non-controversial learning objectives as "cover" for Queer Cult-transformational work.[115] Of course, this is exactly what Freire advised in his critical pedagogy: academic lessons are *mediators* to "political knowledge." For example, one teacher "used an exploration

113 Hermann-Wilmarth, J., & Ryan, C. L. (2018). Navigating parental resistance: Learning from responses of LGBTQ-inclusive elementary school teachers. *Theory Into Practice*, 58(1), 89–98.
114 ibid.
115 ibid.

of 'being problem solvers' as an opportunity to read LGBTQ-inclusive books alongside books about other issues of oppression, such as racism, classism, and sexism."[116] This technique allows radicals to "rationalize" their curriculum choices to parents. That way, if a parent raises concerns about a given topic, the educator can defer to the larger, non-controversial project of "being problem solvers." Being against problem-solving is a difficult position to hold. The goal is to use "strategic" language to make radicalization more "palatable" for parents.

> Linda also chose to explicitly share these frameworks and units with parents at the beginning of the year to inform them of the kinds of texts and approaches she would be using, but she was particular about the words she used to describe them. As she said, "I like the language that [says] teachers... 'teach inclusively.' Because...it helps frame it for parents in a way that is more palatable for anybody who might have an issue.[117] (Hermann-Wilmarth & Ryan, 2019, p. 92)

Queer Activists also use the "authority of their mandated curriculum" to create "cover" for their radical "queer work."[118] That is to say, teachers who want to practice Queer Theory on children can refer to the state-mandated curriculum as a justification for their curricular choices. For example, the authors describe how one teacher "foregrounded traditional literacy skills while asking students to read, write, and research, even when the subject of that work was transgender people's need for access to bathrooms that match their gender identity." Yet again we see Freire. "If a parent argued that she [the teacher] had 'an agenda,'" the authors write, "she knew she could show them how that

---

116   ibid.
117   ibid.
118   ibid.

agenda was centered in her responsibilities to develop students' literacy."[119]

> The high expectation that she had of their literacy skills placed ELA and LGBTQ-inclusive teaching on equal ground. For example, one child's parents had expressed concern about the class reading Alex Gino's *George* (2015) and discussing transgender identities. When that child was working on a project related to the book, Hill asked if he'd had some help. The student nodded slowly and said, "My dad checked my work for commas." Because of Fern's strong focus on ELA skills, parents who might not agree with the LGBTQ-related content could find ways to come to terms with what their child was learning by focusing on ELA skills.[120] (Hermann-Wilmarth & Ryan, 2019, p. 93)

If parents manage to break through the first two layers of deception—strategic manipulations of language and hiding behind mandated curriculum as a "cover for queer work"—then teachers begin punishing parents by proxy, which is to say they attack their children. For instance, the authors recall a parent who did not want their daughter to participate in classroom discussions about transgender books (see *George,* a novel about a "transgender" fourth grader named Melissa). To resolve this egregious level of parental resistance, the teacher told the parents that their daughter could "be in another area" and "read another book or do something else." This strategic maneuver is meant to make the parent bear the weight and responsibility of a child's exclusion. The child likely doesn't fully understand why they can't be in class with their friends, and when that child inevitably questions their teacher as to why they aren't invited to the party,

---

119   ibid.
120   ibid.

the teacher can respond in the exact way you would expect—
"Your mom and dad said you can't join us." Said another way,
Queer Activists are attempting to force parents to make a difficult
choice: Do I protect my kid, which will ultimately confuse them
and alienate them from their peers (driving them away from me
and into the radical's hands), or do I let it happen and hope for
the best? There are other choices, like pulling your children from
a schooling system that is subverting your relationship with your
child while bragging about it in academic journals.

THE MAGIC CIRCLE

Queer Activists hide information, gaslight, and lie to parents
about what schools teach and do with children. They think all
of society is deceptive and actively brainwashing everyone into
normalcy, so, in their mind, they are just doing what everyone
else is doing, but for "good." Queer Theory argues that parents
are a counterrevolutionary force—a means to inculcate children
with normal and stabilizing behaviors and values. Parents are
anathema to the queer educational project, which is why Queer
Activists cloak their practices with manipulative language to
deceive parents and keep the counterrevolutionary forces at bay.
Parents are not offered a "seat at the table"[121] in queer classrooms.

Queer Activists will lie to you and tell you that they must
create an "inclusive" classroom to support gay and lesbian kids.
Queer Theory has nothing to do with being gay or lesbian. Recall
David Halperin's words in the act of defining "queer": "*Unlike
gay identity* [emphasis added], which, though deliberately pro-
claimed in an act of affirmation, is nonetheless rooted in the

---

121   Torres, J. T., & Ferry, N. C. (2019). Not everyone gets a seat at the table!:
Responding to the language games of diversity. In S. Sharma & A. M. Lazar
(Eds.), *Rethinking 21st century diversity in teacher preparation, K–12 education, and
school policy* (pp. 21–37). Springer.

positive fact of homosexual object-choice, queer identity need not be grounded in any positive truth or in any stable reality." Acceptance isn't the goal because acceptance doesn't "require investigating the construction, production, and maintenance of what is considered normative, nor does it challenge the status quo."[122] Acceptance isn't the goal because acceptance would *stabilize*. The goal is *destabilization*. The goal is to provide a *queer education* for *all* children.

> Queer-inclusive education can be described as teaching that demonstrates a commitment to acknowledging sexual and gender identities other than those present in traditional classrooms and curriculum (the heteronormative, gender-normative status quo.) At its best, it moves well beyond LGBTQ-inclusive education (intended to benefit children who may be LGBTQ-identified or from families with an LGBTQ-identified family member) toward an inclusive, critical education for *all* children.[123] (Lin, 2017, p. 2)

You can think of the queer classroom as a magic circle, with the Queer Activist stepping inside and acting as a sorcerer, casting spells and incantations. This magic is designed to capture and orient a child's imagination for revolution. The point of exposing children to the onslaught of signals, warnings, and rituals is to construct a false reality where children lose their ability to perceive the real world. Then, once destabilized and out of touch with reality, the sorcerer introduces a secret, divine knowledge—a bite of the apple—that introduces to the child the idea that they

---

122 Jackson Kellinger, J. (2019). Queer(y)ing teacher education: Ignorance, insecurity, and intolerance. In C. Mayo & N. M. Rodriguez (Eds.), *Queer pedagogies: Theory, praxis, politics* (pp. 109–126). Springer.
123 Lin, C. K. (2017). Changing the Shape of the Landscape: Sexual Diversity Frameworks and the Promise of Queer Literacy Pedagogy in the Elementary Classroom. *Occasional Paper Series*, 2017 (37).

live in a prison that must be destroyed. The prison is society; the prison is the child's mind; the prison is the child's body.

The sorcerer uses the queer classroom to cast spells and brainwash children. She knows that if she can set the stage properly, children will struggle to differentiate between fantasy and reality when they return home. The sorcerers know that "Educators are indeed the administrators of culture,"[124] and educators can radically transform that culture through education. These sorcerers say as much in their literature, and it's time we start paying attention:

> For all the criticism teachers receive for 'indoctrinating' students, turning them into liberal-minded cry-babies, not much has been said in defense. At the very least, a shy denial is made. It is time for educators to own this criticism and admit that is exactly what we do.[125] (Torres & Ferry, 2019, p. 33)

---

124   Torres, J. T., & Ferry, N. C. (2019). Not everyone gets a seat at the table!: Responding to the language games of diversity. In S. Sharma & A. M. Lazar (Eds.), *Rethinking 21st century diversity in teacher preparation, K–12 education, and school policy* (pp. 21–37). Springer.
125   ibid.

Chapter 6

QUEER PEDAGOGY

Monday morning a child brings a stray dog into the classroom.

The traditional teacher sees that it is removed immediately.

The progressive teacher builds on the students' interest; perhaps measures and weighs the animal with the children, has the children draw and write about the dog, and eventually calls the humane society.

The Freirian teacher does what the progressive teacher does but more. She asks questions, using the dog as the object of reflection. "Why are there so many stray dogs in our neighborhood?" "Why are there more here than in the rich suburbs?" "Why do people have dogs?" "Why doesn't the city allocate enough money to clean up after the dogs and care for the strays?" While accepting stray animals into a classroom isn't the bellwether mark of an elementary Freiran [sic] teacher, engaging children in reflective dialogue on topics of their interest is.[126] (Peterson, 2009, p. 305)

---

126 Peterson, R. E. (2009). Teaching how to read the world and change it: Critical pedagogy in the intermediate grades. In A. Darder, M. P. Baltodano, & R. D. Torres (Eds.), *The critical pedagogy reader* (2nd ed., pp. 305–323). Routledge.

You're not likely to find the words "Queer Theory" in your children's curriculum, lesson plans, or homework. Queer Activists aren't teaching kids about Michel Foucault or Judith Butler. They aren't explaining what Queer Theory is, how it developed, or how it reproduces Karl Marx's revolutionary program. Queer Theory isn't taught to children—it is *practiced* on them. Simply put, Queer Activists use the "theory" of Queer Theory to determine what kids should learn, how they should be taught, and what they should do with their education. Queer Activists then put this theory into practice, altering their teaching methods and practices to brainwash children to become Queer Activists.

Throughout the 1960s, '70s, and '80s, North American Marxists (most notably—Michael Apple, Herbert Gintis, Samuel Bowles, and Peter McLaren) used Critical Theory to analyze "how societies reproduce themselves through their school systems and how schools reproduce social injustice by failing to produce a citizenry in which all individuals achieve equal educational outcomes."[127] These Marxists wanted to know how education reproduced a stable, counter-revolutionary capitalist society. The North American Marxist critiques and activism produced during these decades were highly influential in the academy. Still, they failed to answer a crucial question: *How do Marxists stop society from reproducing itself?* As it turns out, the best way to solve the "problem of reproduction" is to hijack education. Enter Paulo Freire.

During the 1960s, while working with peasant farmers in South America, Brazilian Marxist Paulo Freire developed his Critical Theory of education. Critical Pedagogy is the practical application of Freire's theory. Critical Pedagogy is a set of *critical*

---

127   McLaren, P., & Hammer, R. (1989). Critical pedagogy and the postmodern challenge: Towards a critical postmodernist pedagogy of liberation. *Educational Foundations*, 3(3): 29–62. (p. 40).

(Marxist) teaching methods and practices meant to awaken a *critical consciousness* in students.[128] It is a means of teaching children to become Marxists so they will break society rather than reproduce it. Critical Pedagogy is the problem of reproduction solved.

> Freire argues that critical pedagogy focuses on personal liberatory education through the development of critical consciousness. He further argues that liberatory education "raises students' consciousness and prepares them to engage in larger social struggles for liberation." Serving as a catalyst to the commitment of social justice and to the development of a new social order, liberatory education attempts to empower learners to engage in critical dialogue that critiques and challenges oppressive social conditions nationally and globally and to envision and work towards a more just society.[129] (Jean-Marie & Normore & Brooks, 2009, p. 12)

Freire defines critical consciousness as the ability to recognize, analyze, and ultimately eliminate oppression. It involves developing a deep awareness of "systemic power," inequalities, and the interconnectedness of various forms of oppression. If one has critical consciousness, they not only work to understand the world through a Marxist lens—they feel a deep moral impulse to change it. Or, as Marx himself stated in his *Theses on Feuerbach*, "Philosophers have hitherto only interpreted the world in various ways; the point is to change it."[130]

---

128   Freire, P. (2005) *Education for Critical Consciousness.* New York: Continuum International Publishing Group.

129   Jean-Marie, G., Normore, A. H., & Brooks, J. S. (2009). Leadership for Social Justice: Preparing 21st Century School Leaders for a New Social Order. *Journal of Research on Leadership Education,* 4(1).

130   Marx, K. (n.d.). *Theses on Feuerbach.* Retrieved from https://www.Marxists. org/archive/marx/works/1845/theses

During the *Critical Turn in Education*, Marxists imported Freire's methods to the United States, where they picked up Critical Pedagogy and adapted it first for universities (to train future educators) and then for K–12 schools. It is not possible to understand how Queer Theory is practiced on children in K–12 schools nationwide without first understanding what Critical Pedagogy is and how it works because Critical Pedagogy is how one practices Queer Theory in the classroom.

CRITICAL PEDAGOGY

Critical Pedagogy aims to teach children how to become Marxists who practice Critical Theory. This is very different from saying that the goal is to teach children what Marxism is. Paulo Freire designed his program for *consciousness-raising*, not knowledge transmission. Critical Pedagogy doesn't present children with an alternative worldview that they can choose to believe or not to believe. Critical Pedagogy hijacks classroom curriculum, lessons, and instruction to brainwash kids into developing critical consciousness. The point is to "affirm the voices of marginalized students, engage them *critically* [emphasis added], while at the same time assist them in transforming their communities into sites of struggle and resistance."[131]

Again, educators using Critical Pedagogy do this knowingly. As critical whiteness scholar-activist and critical pedagogue Alison Bailey writes,

> Critical pedagogy begins from a different set of assumptions [than critical thinking] rooted in the neo-Marxian literature on critical theory commonly associated with the Frankfurt School. Here, the

---

131 McLaren, P., & Hammer, R. (1989). Critical pedagogy and the postmodern challenge: Towards a critical postmodernist pedagogy of liberation. *Educational Foundations*, 3(3): 29–62. (p. 41).

critical learner is someone who is empowered and motivated to seek justice and emancipation. Critical pedagogy regards the claims that students make in response to social-justice issues not as propositions to be assessed for their truth value, but as expressions of power that function to re-inscribe and perpetuate social inequalities. Its mission is to teach students ways of identifying and mapping how power shapes our understandings of the world. This is the first step toward resisting and transforming social injustices.[132] (Bailey, 2017, p. 882)

Where did these ideas come from? Paulo Freire believed that the educator's primary objective should be to help oppressed people develop literacy. But not literacy as you and I understand it. Freire's *critical literacy* is the ability to *read the world* as a Marxist does. That is to say, *critical literacy* is the ability to *read oppression* that is said to be hidden in all texts, language, and narratives. Critical Pedagogy is the method for developing *critical literacy*, and it accomplishes this by pushing learners to develop a "language of oppression" so that they might speak to their oppressed "standpoint" and become Marxist activists charged with transforming society.

According to Freire, traditional literacy programs are designed to teach learners how to fit into and be successful in the current, oppressive society. He argued that the reading and writing taught in traditional literacy programs is *bourgeois reading and writing*. Freire believed that all teaching is inherently political, and the oppressors in society hide their political project in what they choose to teach and what they count as "approved" or "privileged" ways of reading and writing.

For instance, a learner in a traditional literacy program can be taught to read, write, and define the word "poverty." By

---

132   Bailey, A. (2017). Tracking Privilege-Preserving Epistemic Pushback in Feminist and Critical Race Philosophy Classes. *Hypatia*, 32(4), 876–892. (p. 882)

demonstrating their ability to read, write, and define the word "poverty," the learning objective ends. But Freire would argue that this learner hasn't learned anything other than how to read, write, and define the word "poverty" as the bourgeois ruling class wants them to. For Marxists, you can't read the word "poverty" without *reading the world of* "poverty." The learning objective isn't met until the learner can explain how *poverty* is defined in Marxist terms.

Whereas a traditional literacy program would define "poverty" as "the state of being poor," a *critical literacy* program might define "poverty" as "the state of being *made* poor by an oppressive capitalist system." The bourgeois definition of *poverty* is said to brainwash people into believing that poverty is neutral and natural, and people fall into it for any number of non-conspiratorial reasons. By reading the word "poverty" *critically*, a person is awakened to the Marxist's sociopolitical analysis. To be poor is to be made poor by an unjust system. To be *critically literate* is to read words as a Marxist does and, therefore, to *read the world* as a Marxist does.

Freire believed that entire ideologies (in his case—capitalism and colonialism) are hidden *in the word*, and to learn to read a word is to learn how to decode the ideology hiding within it. For Freire, reading the word—as you and I would understand "reading" to mean—doesn't matter. The only thing that matters is *reading situations* that words represent as a Marxist would.

Freire's entire program aimed to use the cover of "literacy" education to radicalize peasants by teaching them how to become Marxists who practice Critical Theory. It didn't matter if the peasants actually learned how to read or write. The only thing that mattered was teaching peasants how to view and think about the world as a Marxist does. For Freire, literacy lessons were an excuse to use classroom time to radicalize peasants.

Paulo Freire's *critical literacy* program comprises several distinct stages. The initial phase requires teachers to distance themselves from their traditional roles and embrace the position of facilitators and "co-learners" alongside their students. Freire contends that students, which he calls "learners," are already "knowers" of their lived experiences. On the other hand, teachers, occupying positions of privilege rather than oppression, cannot "know" the lived experiences of their learners until those experiences are revealed through Critical Pedagogy. Freire argues that teachers have inherently embraced the dominant bourgeois ideology, whether by subconsciously internalizing it (false consciousness) or by knowingly using it for personal gain. This is evident in their certification within a system that exclusively permits individuals with "approved" or "privileged" knowledge (bourgeois knowledge) to become teachers. To address the inherent privilege associated with teaching, critical literacy programs require teachers to acknowledge that their students possess a deeper understanding of the workings of the world than they do.

Freire argues that oppressed individuals possess a unique perspective, often referred to as "standpoint" or "positionality" in society. They not only comprehend how their oppressors operate but also have firsthand experience of oppression. This "double consciousness" imbues the oppressed with a more elevated and "authentic" form of knowledge, commonly referred to as "lived experience." It gives them a unique insight into how the world works. In acknowledging the unjust power dynamic between teachers and students, Critical Pedagogy urges teachers to relinquish their bourgeois knowledge and authoritative positions. In Freire's program, teachers veer away from conventional teaching methods and adopt a co-teaching and co-learning approach with their students, what he referred to as "the gnostic cycle." Teachers and students enter a classroom of "cosuffering...as they struggle both to transcend and transform the circumstances of their disempowerment."[133]

The second stage of Freire's program involves teachers facilitating (rather than lecturing) open discussions with their students. They guide students in uncovering and developing *their own knowledge*, independent from the influence of their oppressors, promoting a more "transformative" learning experience. This *dialogical model* aims to foster conversations that elicit words, phrases, or stories known as "generative themes" that resonate with the students.

> The generative theme is a topic taken from students' knowledge of their own lived experiences that is compelling and controversial enough to elicit their excitement and commitment. Such themes are saturated with affect, emotion, and meaning because they engage the fears, anxieties, hopes and dreams of both students and their teachers. Generative themes arise at the point where the personal lives of students intersect with the larger society and the globalized world.[134] (Kincheloe, 2008, p. 11)

It's worth reminding the reader here that the authors of *Drag Pedagogy* characterize the presence and performance of a drag queen in classrooms as a *generative* learning opportunity. Freire argued that students learn more when their learning is engaging and relevant to their "lived experience" of oppression. Because of this, Freire advocated for teachers to use classroom conversations to *generate* oppressive themes that they can then latch onto and anchor their lessons. Freire encouraged teachers to push and pull

---

133   McLaren, P., & Hammer, R. (1989). Critical pedagogy and the postmodern challenge: Towards a critical postmodernist pedagogy of liberation. *Educational Foundations*, 3(3): 29–62. (p. 52).
134   Kincheloe, J. L. (2008). *Knowledge and critical pedagogy: An introduction.* Springer.

conversations in a political direction, waiting for their learners to say something that can be tied to oppression, like the word "poverty." Teachers can then incorporate words like "poverty" into their vocabulary lessons, making them more relevant for learners.

The third stage of Paulo Freire's method is to take the words learners find engaging and construct a Marxist political lesson around them—hence the deliberate selection of easily politicized vocabulary terms. The first step in creating this lesson involved "codifying" the chosen vocabulary terms into pictures, graphs, charts, or other visual (even auditory) forms. Freire would show vocabulary terms in written form next to the visual representations of those terms. So, if the word was "poverty," Freire would show the word "poverty" next to a picture of people living in poverty. But the point wasn't to help peasants see something they understood—people in poverty—and then think, "So that's the word to describe this." The point was to use the word "poverty" to launch into a Marxist political analysis of why people end up living in poverty. One can imagine where this is going. The "vocabulary lesson" quickly devolves into a justification for the Marxist to explain that people live in poverty because society is designed to oppress them.

The fourth stage of Freire's process involved "problematizing" the pictures, graphs, and charts by moralizing the images and data to conjure an emotional response from students. This process most often involves asking the learners endless questions to guide them to the understanding that the images represent something morally wrong with how society works. Moralizing the images and data isn't difficult. It's easy to be overwhelmed by pictures of people suffering, and it's easy to confuse illiterate peasants (or children!) using cherry-picked data, oversimplified or deceptive graphs, and emotionally loaded interpretations and descriptions.

The point of problematizing something is to identify a person or group needing saving. Once those people have been identified, the goal is to categorize them as victims. If there are victims, there are wrongdoers and perpetrators. By problematizing an image of "poverty," Freire's method allows Marxists to hijack a student's emotions and use that gut instinct to push learners into *reading situations* as a Marxist does—to push them into splitting the world between the oppressors and the oppressed. That is, problematizing something generates a strong emotional and moral impulse to fight for a team.

The final stage of Freire's practice is *decodification*. In this stage, learners are asked to *identify as victims*. The point of Freire's entire approach, up until this point, is to set the stage—the goal is to use pictures and endless discussions of morality to generate a supercharged, emotional atmosphere where students feel that something must be done to alleviate the suffering of the victims they are looking at. Then, through *decodification*, Freire asks the learners to *identify as the victims* they have spent the entire lesson discussing. Decodification is the process of convincing learners that *they are* the victims in pictures, charts, and stories. The point of decodification is to ask learners to identify with the victims they see—*as victims*—whether by way of skin color, ethnicity, sex, gender, sexuality, or class. Through decodification, learners step onto the stage and join the oppressed in a revolutionary struggle for liberation.

Freire describes the overall process of Critical Pedagogy as teaching people how to practice *critical reflection*, which generates *critical motivation* and then *critical action*. Critical reflection is reflecting on the world through the lens of Critical Theory. This generates a strong moral impulse—*critical motivation*—to do something. This critical motivation leads to *critical action*—activism informed and prescribed by Critical Theory. By moving from critical reflection to critical motivation and then to critical action, one develops critical consciousness.

Critical Pedagogy is a set of Marxist teaching methods and practices that push learners to develop critical consciousness. Critical consciousness is the Marxist belief that everything in society is designed to oppress you, and the only way to see "the truth" about the world is to become a Marxist who practices Critical Theories to denounce the sources of oppression in the world. If you recall, a Critical Theory has three components: a Marxist's idealized version of society, a Marxist's critique of our current society, and Marxist activism to move from our current society to the idealized version. So, Freire's Critical Pedagogy pushes learners to believe that all of society is designed to oppress them, it brainwashes them to think only Marxists know "the truth" about how the world works, and it inspires them to do political activism to transform their world. It is a method of *thought reform*.

QUEER PEDAGOGY

Paulo Freire's methods and practices dominate the U.S. educational landscape. When educators talk of making lessons and curriculum "more engaging," they are doing so because they have been programmed to believe that Freire's methods are common-sense "good teaching." Likewise, when educators say, "learners need to see themselves in the curriculum," they might not understand that "see themselves" reliably translates to "see themselves as victims." The people who spread Freire's methods throughout the U.S. and Canada in the 1980s knew well what they were doing. But many today don't know where their pedagogy, which is *critical*, comes from because they are a few steps removed from Freire himself. Freire's practices were picked up and diffused by thousands, so a college student learning to be a teacher today learns how to practice Critical Pedagogy without necessarily studying Freire explicitly (although many do). Future educators now learn Culturally Relevant Teaching as they are prepared to "interrupt common-sense ways of seeing the world" and "act against ideological and institutional processes and forms that reproduce oppressive conditions."[135]

Queer Activists use Freire's methods and practices to teach children how to become Queer Activists. Queer Pedagogy (Queer Theory + Critical Pedagogy) is Critical Pedagogy informed and directed by Queer Theory. Queer Theory is the motivation—the unique insight into how the world works. Queer Theory is the "truth" of the world—Critical Pedagogy is the technique and method for revealing this truth to others.

> Queer pedagogy, grounded in critical theory, introduces ways to challenge biases, assumptions, and customary ways of thinking about traditionally "fixed" categories of sexuality and gender. It challenges us to radically examine and redefine how we think about and conceptualize the act of teaching, our notions and practices of knowledge, and formal and informal curriculum. To queer is to destabilize the social, cultural, and political normalizing structures that work to solidify identities and in doing so skew power toward the "norm."[136] (Dunne, 2017, p. 42)

Queer Pedagogy is a collection of methods and practices that Queer Activists use to hijack regular classroom instruction to

---

135   Gottesman, I. (2016). *The critical turn in education: From Marxist critique to poststructuralist feminism to critical theories of race* (1st ed.). Routledge. (p. xii).
136   Burnes, T. R., & Stanley, J. L. (Eds.). (2017). *Teaching LGBTQ psychology: Queering innovative pedagogy and practice.* American Psychological Association.

groom kids into becoming Queer Activists. Whereas traditional teaching creates order out of chaos, Queer Pedagogy "creates chaos out of order."[137] It is "risky and explosive," requiring "a radical interrogation of all social analyses, particularly in areas that appear to have little to do with sex."[138] Queer Pedagogy "assumes a diligence to actively and intentionally model ways that redefine or invoke questions about meanings and concepts that serve to reinforce characterizations of 'normal' and perpetuate societal binaries."[139] Queer Pedagogy is the reason children across the United States can't go a day in school without having sex, gender, sexuality, and victimhood shoved in their faces. None of this is an accident. Again, I turn to an example from the literature to clarify these points.

Queering Critical Literacy and Numeracy for Social Justice is a book that explains how one Queer Activist is using Queer Pedagogy in her 5th and 6th-grade classrooms to teach mathematics. As the title implies, this Queer Activist isn't teaching math— she is teaching math *for* social justice, just as Freire taught "literacy" for "liberation." Like all Critical Educators, the author thinks math is inherently political and can either be used to conserve the current society or dismantle it. What this means, in practice, is that math isn't the focus of the course at all—"learning to do math" is the motte. The author uses her *Math for a*

---

137 Jackson Kellinger, J. (2019). Queer(y)ing teacher education: Ignorance, insecurity, and intolerance. In C. Mayo & N. M. Rodriguez (Eds.), *Queer pedagogies: Theory, praxis, politics* (pp. 109–126). Springer.

138 Rands, K. (2019). Mathematical Inqueery: Queering the theory, praxis, and politics of mathematics pedagogy. In *Queer pedagogies: Theory, praxis, politics* (pp. 59–74). Springer.

139 Burnes, T. R., & Stanley, J. L. (Eds.). (2017). *Teaching LGBTQ psychology: Queering innovative pedagogy and practice.* American Psychological Association. (p. 43).

Cause course to teach students to read and do math *for* Social Justice, which includes Queer Activism.

Rather than learning to do math, middle school students in *Math for a Cause* ranked social justice topics (education, the environment, health care, or same-sex marriage) and "were tasked with creating a narrower focus within that topic, choosing their own articles, and then creating their math problems from their reading and research."[140]

> During the second unit…Jimmy Smith (a fifth-grade boy) found a report on transgender patients' experiences with healthcare services and his group decided to use this to create their math problem. The group discussed things about the report that surprised them, such as transgender people facing discrimination from doctors and reporting that they did not feel comfortable visiting the doctor even for things unrelated to their gender, such as flu. The group asked me why doctors would discriminate against their patients: This was a foreign concept to my group of cisgender middle schoolers, whose school advocated for kindness and inclusion. Why would a doctor possibly discriminate against a patient, they wondered? We had a long conversation about what this discrimination may look like…The students were beginning to understand the subtle ways transphobic discrimination could occur.[141] (Pennell, 2019, p. 64)

The Queer Activist who taught *Math for a Cause* used focus groups and individual conversations with students—the Freirean *dialogical* model—to fish for *generative themes* that piqued student interest. After identifying topics that each student found "engaging," facilitators split the class into research groups

---

140   Pennell, S. M. (2019). *Queering critical literacy and numeracy for social justice: Navigating the course.* Palgrave Macmillan. (p. 55).
141   ibid.

tasked with reading articles about the topic and creating a "mathematical question inspired from the article."[142] The articles were either chosen by the teacher or selected by the students after their teacher reviewed them. In effect, these articles served as *codifications* of oppression—they all included perceived victims of social injustice.

After reading and studying the articles, the teacher *decodified* them with her students. Jimmy's group had discrimination "revealed" to them as something that not only exists but is hidden in everyday interactions between some people who have power and others who don't. By decodifying the articles, the teacher was modeling the theory and practice of Queer Theory to her students. In effect, the teacher invited students to enter into her conspiratorial worldview and asked them to start *understanding themselves in relation to oppression.*

> As they read, they completed scaffolded handouts that focused on *critical literacy* [emphasis added] by asking them to answer questions such as "Who has the power?". After this, they would brainstorm and create a mathematical question inspired from the article and conduct more research as needed…Often, the math portion was difficult as the students had to sift through data and try to "read" the numbers. As such, students did not usually finish their math problems.[143] (Pennell, 2019, p. 22)

Math for a Cause should be thought of as nothing more than a brainwashing program to push kids to become Marxists who practice Critical Theory—in this case, Queer Theory. Learning to do math wasn't *really* the learning objective—learning to *read the world critically through math* was. The focus questions that the

---

142   ibid. (p. 22)
143   ibid .

teacher provided to students to guide their reading of the articles make this clear:

- What/who does the author write as having the POWER? How do you know?
- What are the BELIEFS of the author? How do you know?
- Based on the power and beliefs, who do you think is the intended AUDIENCE?
- In this article, what do the author or people interviewed see as NORMAL? How do you know?
- What math words do you notice (value, weight) and how does that effect [sic] the meaning?
- Are the opinions in the article different from your own? How?
- What is your reaction to the article? (How do you feel reading it?)
- What do you want readers of this article to know about the topic?[144]

Queer Pedagogy is not at all concerned with teaching children how to read, write, or do math. Teaching children how to develop their queer literacy (Queer Theory + critical literacy) "defies notions of common sense because it does not aim even to understand that which is being read."[145] As the author of *Queering Critical Literacy and Numeracy for Social Justice* makes clear, the students "did not usually finish their math problems." Queer Pedagogy is entirely concerned with "trouble[ing] the very

---

144   ibid.
145   Kumashiro, K. (2002). *Troubling education: "Queer" activism and anti-oppressive pedagogy*. Routledge. (p. 78).

idea of 'normal,'"[146] confusing "our ways of talking about and understanding things,"[147] and using typical reading and math lessons as cover for political brainwashing. As the author of *Queering Critical Literacy and Numeracy for Social Justice* writes, "Queer Pedagogy is primarily concerned with *critically* [emphasis added] examining and deconstructing heteronormativity and the other boundaries and limits surrounding schooling."[148] Additional Queer Theory literature reveals the goal of Queer Pedagogy more precisely. As Hackford-Peer explicitly states in *"That wasn't very free thinker": Queer critical pedagogy in the early grades*, the goal of Queer Pedagogy is to:

> create classrooms where teachers and students can work toward a kind of queer conscientization where students and teachers "achieve a deepening awareness of the [ways that heteronormative discourses and socio-cultural practices]…shape their lives and [grapple with] their own capacities to [undo] and re-create."[149] (Hackford-Peer, 2019, p. 79)

Queer Activists *queer* normal teaching practices—normal, as in, actually teaching kids to read and do math!—to *conscientize* (push them to develop *critical consciousness*) children. Math lessons become endless discussions of gender, sex, sexuality, and *injustice*. Reading lessons become nothing more than learning

---

146   Linville, D. (Ed.). (2017). Queering education: Pedagogy, curriculum, policy. *Occasional Paper Series 37*. Bank Street College of Education.

147   McCann, H., & Monaghan, W. (2019). *Queer Theory now: From foundations to futures*. Bloomsbury Publishing. (p. 8).

148   Pennell, S. M. (2019). *Queering critical literacy and numeracy for social justice: Navigating the course*. Palgrave Macmillan. (p. 36).

149   Hackford-Peer, K. (2019). "That wasn't very free thinker": Queer critical pedagogy in the early grades. In C. Mayo & N. M. Rodriguez (Eds.), *Queer Pedagogies: Theory, Praxis, Politics* (pp. 75–92). Critical Studies of Education (Vol. 11, S. R. Steinberg, Series Ed.). Springer.

how to practice Queer Theory to determine who in society has power and who doesn't. The point is to radicalize children by revealing "the truth" of their oppression through "math" and "reading" lessons.

CRISIS AND SOCIAL-EMOTIONAL LEARNING

Queer Pedagogy is a method of teaching that intentionally thrusts children into crisis, and the people who practice it in classrooms know this. Queer Activists believe that "entering crisis…is a required and desired part of learning."[150] They believe this because they think that students must be shocked out of the "harmful repetition" of oppressive norms in their classrooms.[151]

> Repeating what is already learned can be comforting and therefore desirable; students' learning things that question their knowledge and identities can be emotionally upsetting. For example, suppose students think society is meritocratic but learn that it is racist, or think that they themselves are not contributing to homophobia but learn that in fact they are. In such situations, students learn that the ways they think and act are not only limited but also oppressive. Learning about oppression and about the ways they often unknowingly comply with oppression can lead students to feel paralyzed with anger, sadness, anxiety, and guilt; it can lead to a form of emotional crisis.[152] (Kumashiro, 2002, p. 74)

Pushing children into personal crisis is a necessary component of Queer Pedagogy because it "spur[s] students to work for positive

---

150 Kumashiro, K. K. (2002). Against repetition: Addressing resistance to anti-oppressive change in the practices of learning, teaching, supervising, and researching. *Harvard Educational Review*, 72(1). (p. 74).

151 ibid.

152 ibid.

social change."[153] Crisis is required to destabilize and dislodge a child's desire to be normal, which manifests as "entrenched resistance"[154] to the political activism Queer Theory requires of them. In other words that echo Freire's, crisis is the engine of the *queer gnostic* cycle. For Queer Pedagogy to work, children must be hammered emotionally so that they might desire activism rather than "normalcy." The process is "violent and disruptive" because "it endeavors to disrupt some deeply entrenched 'truths' and taken-for-granted assumptions, beliefs, values, and practices."[155] It's easier to brainwash a child into a cult when they are an emotional wreck, experiencing an "uncomfortable disequilibrium for which they are unprepared."[156] The instability and confusion are intentional—a crumbling foundation is a precondition of the whole project.[157]

Identity is *the* lever of crisis in queer classrooms. Queer Activists use the cover of math and reading lessons to "proliferate identifications" and introduce children to the smorgasbord of identities they have to choose from, each with positive or negative valence underwriting it, as defined by intersectionality and Queer Theory. The point of introducing kids to a taste of the rainbow is to get children to identify with a position from which

153   Pennell, S. M. (2019). *Queering critical literacy and numeracy for social justice: Navigating the course.* Palgrave Macmillan. (p. 40).

154   Kumashiro, K. (2002). *Troubling education: "Queer" activism and anti-oppressive pedagogy.* Routledge. (p. 48).

155   Steinberg, S. R., & Down, B. (Eds.). (2020). *The SAGE Handbook of Critical Pedagogies* (Three Volume Set). SAGE Publications Ltd. (p. xliv).

156   McLean, J. (2020). Critical pedagogy: Negotiating the nuances of implementation. In S. R. Steinberg & B. Down (Eds.), *The SAGE Handbook of Critical Pedagogies* (Three Volume Set) (pp. 236–253). SAGE Publications Ltd. (p. 248).

157   Kumashiro, K. K. (2002). Against repetition: Addressing resistance to anti-oppressive change in the practices of learning, teaching, supervising, and researching. *Harvard Educational Review*, 72(1).

they can attack normalcy. Said another way, the point of asking a child to pick up various identities is to remove that child from the "normal" category so the educator can *position them against it.* Queer Activists use Queer Pedagogy to maneuver children into "alternative sites of identification and critique"[158] so that those children will begin to question who they are. By convincing kids that identities like "non-binary" and "gender-fluid" are real, Queer Activists "unsettle the myth of normalcy as an originary state."[159]

Simply put, Queer Activists convince kids that they can't identify as normal boys or girls—they must choose *political positions* and enter into an *identity crisis.* Queer Activists must first persuade kids to see themselves as different by "forc[ing] a separation of their sense of self from a sense of normalcy."[160] They are then led to feel as though they are oppressed because they're abnormal. Only then can kids be taught the key reversal that activates them: that they are abnormal *because* they are oppressed. That is, they would be "normal" too if it weren't for society's expectations to be normal on other terms. Society, by failing to accommodate their quirks, is making them abnormal.

> Once in a crisis, a student can go in many directions, some that may lead to anti-oppressive change, others that may lead to more entrenched resistance. Therefore, educators have a responsibility not only to draw students into a possible crisis, but also to structure experiences that can help them work through their crises productively.[161] (Kumashiro, 2002, pp. 74–75)

---

158   Britzman, D. P. (1998). *Lost Subjects, Contested Objects: Toward a Psychoanalytic Inquiry of Learning.* State University of New York Press. (p. 80).
159   ibid (p. 81)
160   Kumashiro, K. (2002). *Troubling education: "Queer" activism and anti-oppressive pedagogy.* Routledge. (p. 44).
161   Kumashiro, K. K. (2002). Against repetition: Addressing resistance to

This is *not* education. This is *thought reform*. This is systematized *brainwashing*.

Admittedly, the preceding is a difficult concept to understand, but it is the key concept that unlocks the *critical* mindset. It is most visible not in Queer Theory, but in disability studies, which has shared ideas and structure with Queer Theory for decades. Under what is called the "social model of disability," interpreted critically, people with disabilities are not believed to be disabled by their disabilities; they are disabled by society failing to fully accommodate their disabilities to the point where those disabilities are irrelevant to day-to-day life. That is, disabled people are *disabled because they are oppressed* by an ableist society that fails to fully accommodate them (because they wouldn't lack ability if fully accommodated). It is *society's* fault. This is the critically conscious mentality in Queer Theory as well. The "queer" is only abnormal because society defines and oppresses abnormality. This shift in mindset seems subtle (and crazy) but isn't. It's the justification to transform society so that it fully accommodates the Critical Activist.

The queer gnostic cycle is driven by an induced crisis that leads children into criticality. Social and Emotional Learning (SEL) is the tool that Queer Activists use to help students work through their manufactured identity crisis "productively." SEL provides the "space in [the] curriculum in which students can work through crisis" and move from "being stuck and into a different intellectual, emotional, and political space."[162]

According to *CASEL* (The Collaborative for Academic, Social, and Emotional Learning), "SEL is the process through which all young people and adults acquire and apply the

---

anti-oppressive change in the practices of learning, teaching, supervising, and researching. *Harvard Educational Review*, 72(1).

162   ibid.

knowledge, skills, and attitudes to develop healthy identities, manage emotions and achieve personal and collective goals, feel and show empathy for others, establish and maintain supportive relationships, and make responsible and caring decisions."[163] CASEL's *Transformative SEL* program is the most popular SEL program implemented in schools today. It's also one of the primary tools that Queer Activists use to "help" students manage their induced crisis.

As described by CASEL, SEL programs are meant to be *transformative*, as in *causing a marked change in the consciousness* of children. SEL programs are said to help students develop character and cope with emotions in a healthy and positive manner so that they may enter the classroom prepared to learn. What CASEL and other SEL advocates don't tell you in their colorful marketing materials is that all of this "character development" and "emotional regulation" is situated in a *critical* context. That is, SEL pushes children to develop their character and identity through the lens of Queer Theory. When you look under the cover of CASEL's *Transformative SEL* program, you find the same Marxist engine that you see everywhere else in U.S. education.

Indeed, according to SEL guru Linda Darling-Hammond, writing in the foreword to the *Handbook of Social and Emotional Learning: Research and Practice*, Social-Emotional Learning is based on the "transformative" and "humanizing" Marxist methods of Paulo Freire:

> As Paulo Freire explained, humanization is "the process of becoming more fully human as social, historical, thinking, communicating, transformative, creative persons who participate in and with the

---

163   Jagers, R. J., Rivas-Drake, D., & Williams, B. (2019). Transformative social and emotional learning (SEL): Toward SEL in service of educational equity and excellence. *Educational Psychologist*, 54(3), 162–184.

world." Educators, he argued, must "listen to their students and build on their knowledge and experiences in order to engage in… personalized educational approaches that further the goals of humanization and transformation." Indeed, this is what we see in schools that successfully undertake the journey of becoming socially and emotionally educative. (Durlak et al., 2015, p. xii)[164]

According to the CASEL publication *Transformative Social and Emotional Learning (SEL): Toward SEL in Service of Educational Equity and Excellence*:

Transformative SEL represents an as-yet underutilized approach that SEL researchers and practitioners can use if they seek to effectively address issues such as power, privilege, prejudice, discrimination, social justice, empowerment, and self-determination… it must cultivate in them [students] the knowledge, attitudes, and skills required for *critical* [emphasis added] examination and collaborative action to address root causes of inequities.[165]

When marketing to educators, CASEL presents a straightforward solution to help mitigate classroom behavioral issues and improve academic achievement. This sales pitch is the motte that everyone buys into. In practice, CASEL's Transformative SEL Framework is a radical program that uses a child's induced emotional crisis as leverage to brainwash them. The "critical examination," referenced in the quotation above, means *Critical Theory*. The "collaborative action to address root causes of inequities" means *activism*. CASEL's

---

164   Durlak, J. A., Domitrovich, C. E., Weissberg, R. P., & Gullotta, T. P. (Eds.) (2015). *Handbook of Social and Emotional Learning: Research and Practice*. Guilford Press.

165   Jagers, R. J., Rivas-Drake, D., & Williams, B. (2019). Transformative social and emotional learning (SEL): Toward SEL in service of educational equity and excellence. *Educational Psychologist*, 54(3), 162–184.

program is *critical* and *transformative*, just like Paulo Freire's Critical Pedagogy and Queer Theory's Queer Pedagogy.

CASEL's framework is less about learning and more about *leverage*. For instance, CASEL's self-awareness competency requires "the ability to recognize one's own biases; to understand the links between one's personal and collective history and identities; and to recognize how thoughts, feelings, and actions are interconnected in and across diverse contacts." So, a child who is becoming self-aware is a child who is coming to terms with the fact that they have biases, as understood by Queer Theory. Likewise, children who are becoming self-aware are learning that they have various identities, that their classmates have various identities, and that they must understand their thoughts, feelings, and actions in relation to these identities in specific *critical* ways. Queer Activists use this competency to push students to become self-aware in the new "revealed" world they now find themselves in—a world in which boys can become girls, girls can become boys, drag queens are celebrated, biology is oppression, and being even slightly uncomfortable with yourself or your body is a likely sign that you are queer and unaware of it. In effect, Queer Activists say, "I know you're uncomfortable now that we've inverted your world, but it's OK. We can help you become more self-aware so you can finally understand who you truly are."

CASEL's self-management competency works the same way. According to CASEL, learning to self-manage is learning "appropriate expressiveness, perseverance, and being agentic in addressing personal and group-level challenges to achieve self- and collectively defined goals and objectives." In other words, learning to self-manage is learning how to behave in the new identity that your Queer Activist teacher has situated you and/ or your classmates into. If being self-aware is learning that you're not normal—you're *queer*—then self-management is learning how to manage your new queer political identity and those of your peers. Teaching children to self-manage, in this context, is to teach them how to manage their emotional crises in such a way that they are more likely to emerge as disciplined activists who can achieve collectivist objectives.

Queer Pedagogy places children into a personal and social crisis. Whereas CASEL's self-awareness and self-management competencies push children to manage their crisis personally, CASEL's social-awareness competency pushes them to manage their crisis in a social context. Social-awareness "involves understanding social norms for constructing behavior in diverse interpersonal and institutional settings." Transformative social-awareness takes one's *critical* self-analysis and uses it as a basis for "*critical* [emphasis added] social analysis." In other words, developing a child's social-awareness is teaching that child how normalcy conditions and determines a group's behaviors and outcomes. Social-awareness is meant to comfort a child by telling them that there are specific ways they can *read the world* to make sense of how people treat them. In effect, social-awareness is the process of taking a child standing in the deconstructed rubble of their old *normal* world—a place they have been taught is full of evil spirits and wickedness—and placing them in the loving embrace of revealed queer wisdom.

According to CASEL, "competence in the relationship skills domain includes the interpersonal sensibilities and facility needed to establish and maintain healthy and rewarding relationships and to effectively navigate settings with differing social and cultural norms and demands." The relationship skills competence thus combines self-awareness, self-management, and social-awareness to ensure that students build "healthy" queer relationships with their peers and teachers. Any beliefs your child holds that disagrees with or is made uncomfortable by Queer

Theory or its practice will have to be suppressed or changed to foster "healthy," "safe," and "inclusive" relationships where every Queer Activist *feels like they belong*. That is, your child will have to accommodate everything Queer Activists throw at them in the name of "relationship skills."

CASEL's responsible decision-making competency "requires the ability to *critically* [emphasis added] examine ethical standards, safety concerns, and behavioral norms for risky behavior; to make realistic evaluations of benefits and consequences of various interpersonal and institutional relationships and actions; and to always make primary collective health and well-being." To build responsible decision-making competence, students must use Queer Theory to critique their school, familial, and community relationships. Queer Theory sets the ethical standards; Queer Theory determines what is considered "safe" or "risky" behavior; Queer Theory determines what "realistic evaluations" look like; and Queer Theory demands the "collective" replace the individual. Responsible students are thus only considered responsible when they become Queer Activists.

CASEL sets the standards and benchmarks for the SEL programs that dominate our schools. CASEL's Transformative SEL is a radical brainwashing program that explicitly calls for students to develop *critical consciousness* and become activists. SEL surveys and lessons allow educators to data-mine children for *generative themes* and *social and emotional leverage points* so that they can then launch into political brainwashing sessions, as outlined by Paulo Freire. Children are bombarded with questions about their identity, sexuality, insecurities, fears, and anxieties. The point is to use Queer Pedagogy, often facilitated directly through SEL, to push children into crisis, generate emotional responses and use those responses as leverage to start using the lens of Queer Theory to reflect on and, ultimately, radically change their lives. Or, as the highly influential "anti-oppressive" educator and Queer Activist Kevin Kumashiro explains, "queer teaching always works through crisis...the goal is to continue teaching and learning through crisis—to continue experiencing the queer."[166]

A final twist to this terrible story is that the crises induced by Queer Activists and SEL themselves will then be used as an excuse for *more SEL and Queer Activism*. The survey data collected will reflect children in identity crises, which Queer Activism intentionally drives, and the prescribed remedy to that crisis is given as more Social-Emotional Learning. The "gnostic cycle" of Social-Emotional Learning, then, is using Social-Emotional Learning to traumatize students and then using their trauma as the justification for more Social-Emotional Learning. In other words, Social-Emotional Learning is classic snake oil.

QUEER CONSCIOUSNESS

The point of Paulo Freire's *critical* teaching practices was to raise a critical consciousness in peasant farmers in Brazil so they would become Marxist revolutionaries. The point of Queer Pedagogy is to raise a queer consciousness in children so they will become Queer Marxist revolutionaries. The point of both of these approaches is, as Freire put it, *perpetual* cultural revolution. Queer Activists have combined Paulo Freire's methods with Queer Theory to generate teaching practices that "reveal the truth" of Queer Theory to kids. Our nation's classrooms no longer focus on cultivating reading and math proficiency. They focus on manipulating a child's natural curiosity and emotions with revolutionary intentions. Children nationwide are relentlessly data mined through social and emotional surveys so that Queer Activists can find the right

---

166   Kumashiro, K. K. (2009). *Against Common Sense: Teaching and Learning Toward Social Justice* (2nd ed.). Routledge. (p. 55).

hook to sink into them. You won't find the words "Queer Theory" in many schools, but the evidence of its presence is undeniable.

Queer Pedagogy is the problem of reproduction solved. Queer Activists believe that traditional phonics programs and multiplication tables stabilize society. They think that learning to read, write, and do math in a normal and neutral way is impossible, so everyone should teach children how to read and do math *for* "social justice," as they define it. Queer Activists think that the purpose of education is to teach children to *read the word so that they can read the world* and change it through revolution. Learning to do math now requires learners to ignore math while focusing on locating and eliminating oppression. Learning to read no longer requires learners to practice reading—it requires them to practice reading the "unstated dominant ideologies hidden between the sentences."[167] In other words, learning to read means developing *critical literacy* so that they may develop a "language of oppression" to use in their war against *normalcy*.

None of what's happening in children's classrooms is normal anymore. Queer Activists have queered education, so parents have difficulty figuring out what is happening in schools. Educators openly admit to lying to the public about what they are doing. Take, for instance, this passage taken from the book *Queer Pedagogies: Theory, Praxis, Politics*:

> I'd like to begin by considering the use of the word *critical* [emphasis added] to describe pedagogy as it has essentially become one of many *code words* [emphasis added] used to make the political agenda of a course invisible or at least less visible. This has allowed educators to access public resources in order to further the goals of social justice in education.[168] (Hackford-Peer, 2019, p. 80)

---

167   Kincheloe, J. L. (2008). *Critical pedagogy primer*. Peter Lang. (p. 16).
168   Hackford-Peer, K. (2019). "That wasn't very free thinker": Queer critical

A parent reads an assignment and sees a weird statistics problem. "Sure," she thinks—"the statistics lesson includes research related to discrimination based on 'gender identity,' which is weird, but the point of the assignment is to help my child learn how to calculate proportionality." Parents see "Social and Emotional Learning" and think, "I'm so glad my kid's school is focusing on character development and resiliency." A child's mom and dad ask, "What did you learn at school today, kiddo?" and their child responds, "I learned that we should include everyone." Understanding Queer Pedagogy allows one to see through the motte and understand the bailey. Education is no longer about equipping children with the knowledge and tools needed to succeed in society. Education is now a political brainwashing program that destabilizes a child's identity and intentionally places them into a crisis. "Ideally, what results from working through crisis is a change in the relationship students see between themselves and the binary of normalcy/Otherness."[169] In other words, Queer Activists manufacture the crisis and use cult techniques to push children to *abolish normalcy*. The learning objective is cultural revolution. The "project of education" has become "the gathering grounds for deconstructive revolts."[170] It's all religious cult child abuse.

pedagogy in the early grades. In C. Mayo & N. M. Rodriguez (Eds.), *Queer Pedagogies: Theory, Praxis, Politics* (pp. 75–92). Critical Studies of Education (Vol. 11, S. R. Steinberg, Series Ed.). Springer.

169   Kumashiro, K. (2002). *Troubling education: "Queer" activism and anti-oppressive pedagogy*. Routledge. (p. 64).

170   Britzman, D. P. (2012). Queer Pedagogy and Its Strange Techniques. In *Counterpoints: Vol. 367, Sexualities in Education: A Reader* (pp. 292–308). Peter Lang AG.

Chapter 7

QUEERING DEVELOPMENTAL PSYCHOLOGY (QUEER CULT PSYCHOLOGY)

What's happening in queer classrooms is unacceptable and should be considered criminally so in many cases. Queer Pedagogy is cult brainwashing. Intentionally placing children into crisis is child abuse. Toss in the pornographic and hyper-sexualized content found in books like *It's Perfectly Normal*,[171] *Gender Queer*,[172] *This Book is Gay*,[173] *Let's Talk About It*,[174] and *Jack of Hearts (And Other*

---

171   Harris, R. H., & Emberley, M. (2009). *It's perfectly normal: a book about changing bodies, growing up, sex and sexual health.* 3rd ed. Candlewick Press.

172   Kobabe, M., & Kobabe, P. (2020). *Gender queer: a memoir.* Portland, OR, Oni Press.

173   Dawson, J., & Gerrell, S. (2015). *This book is gay.* Sourcebooks.

174   Moen, E., & Nolan, M. (2021). *Let's talk about it: the teen's guide to sex, relationships, and being a human.* First edition. Random House Graphic.

Parts)[175] and you have a recipe for what can only be described as sexual cult grooming.

For years, much of Queer Education, especially the queer consciousness-raising methods found in Queer Pedagogy, has remained hidden under a thin veneer of cult slogans, code words, and lies. Understandably, parents have had a difficult time putting together the pieces. That all changed when moms started looking into their school libraries.

Reporting for *City Journal* in May of 2023, Dave Seminara flipped through a few of the "banned books" the mainstream media has been kicking and screaming about. It's inconceivable that any adult would knowingly want their children to have access to pornographic materials in schools. Each of the books Seminara exposed in his piece *Have You Looked Inside Any of These Books?* are too much for many readers, so I'll spare repetition and stick to a single quotation:

> *Jack of Hearts (and Other Parts)* by L.C. Rosen details the "unapologetically queer" sex life of a teenager in graphic detail. The book's dust jacket says, "It's true that Jack has a LOT of sex and he's not ashamed of it." The book is full of pornographic content. "Big hairy muscled men love taking it up the *ss . . . And slim, makeup-wearing types? We love to f*ck and, in my case, getting f*cked too." (Page 111) On page 285, a boy character says, "What I really get turned on by, is the idea of hurting (girls). Not like beating them or anything but spanking them, slapping them, making them wear collars and ball gags and ordering them around." In a rave review, School Library Journal called this disturbing book "an essential addition to library collections that serve teens," recommending it for children in grades ten and up. (The journal also later featured the

175   Rosen, L. C., & Swaab, N. (2018). *Jack of hearts (and other parts)*. First edition. Brown and Company.

book in a column about "delectable dramas for teens" and a feature on "56 excellent books.")[176] (Seminara, 2023)

What's happening in school libraries isn't surprising. The sitting president of the American Library Association (ALA), Emily Drabinski, is a self-described "Marxist lesbian," which should not be taken as a statement of essential identity but of being a Marxist Queer Activist. Drabinski knows what Queer Theory is, as evidenced by her 2013 publication *Queering the Catalog: Queer Theory and the Politics of Correction.*[177] In *Queering the Catalog,* Drabinski argues that librarians should ditch traditional classification methods in favor of *queer* classification methods. What this suggests, in short, is that Drabinski thinks librarians should fill their shelves with Queer Cult propaganda and organize the catalog to direct people to it. Queer Activists like Drabinski have been queering school libraries for a long time, which is why children now have access to pornographic materials—*in school*—nationwide.

As parents wake up to the fact that their children are receiving a queer education, many are asking themselves: *How are the schools justifying this insanity? How are they getting away with psychologically abusing children and exposing minors to pornographic content? How is any of this appropriate in any way?* The short but deep answer to these questions is this: Queer Activists queered developmental psychology and, therefore, they queered what society considers "developmentally appropriate."

176   Seminara, D. (2023, May 17). *Have You Looked Inside Any of These Books?* City Journal. https://www.city-journal.org/article/have-you-looked-inside-any-of-these-books
177   Drabinski, E. (2013). Queering the Catalog: Queer Theory and the Politics of Correction. *Library Quarterly: Information, Community, Policy,* 83(2), 94–111.

QUEER CULT PSYCHOLOGY

The American Academy of Child and Adolescent Psychiatry (AACAP) is "the leading national professional medical association dedicated to treating and improving the quality of life for children, adolescents, and families" affected by mental, behavioral, or developmental disorders.[178] Roughly eight-thousand child and adolescent psychologists are AACAP members, all required to follow the AACAP's code of ethics and practice guidelines. This is a serious problem because the AACAP, like every other cog in the medical-industrial complex, has been colonized by Queer Theory.

Queer Activists captured the AACAP long ago. However, it wasn't until some parents realized what was happening in their children's schools that the organization started placing the depth of its *queer* color on full display. In 2022, the AACAP rushed to the defense of the Madison Metropolitan School District (MMSD) in Wisconsin. Fourteen parents sued the district in 2020, arguing that MMSD's *Guidance & Policies to Support Transgender, Non-binary & Gender Expansive Students* violated their parental rights. The court battle was arduous and the case was ultimately dismissed, at which point the plaintiffs motioned for the Wisconsin Supreme Court to review. The AACAP jumped into the fray, submitting an amicus brief and informing the Wisconsin Supreme Court of the "well accepted psychiatric guidance"[179] related to the MMSD's policies. The AACAP's briefing was chock-full of cult propaganda, including the argument that the MMSD's secretive "social transition" policies "can have

---

178 American Academy of Child and Adolescent Psychiatry. (n.d.). *Home.* Retrieved from https://www.aacap.org/

179 American Academy of Child and Adolescent Psychiatry, & Wisconsin Council of Child and Adolescent Psychiatry. (2022). *Brief of Amicus Curiae.* In The Supreme Court of Wisconsin (Case No. 2020AP1032). Retrieved from https://acefiling.wicourts.gov/document/eFiled/2020AP001032/503742

a significant positive effect on students' futures and outcomes by providing a supportive environment for all students, including those who do not feel they are safe to explore their gender identity at home."[180]

The Wisconsin Supreme Court ultimately denied a motion to review the case, a decision celebrated by the American Civil Liberties Union (ACLU):

> [The dismissal] brings a welcome conclusion to a protracted and arduous legal battle over the ability of Madison Metropolitan School District students to freely and safely explore their identities on their terms, and we are glad that trans and nonbinary students will continue to have the ability to express themselves at school, without fear of being involuntarily outed by staff.[181]

The ACLU's statement is revealing and requires a brief examination to expose a wicked motte and bailey. Let's linger on that last clause: "without fear of being involuntarily outed by staff." What does that mean? It obviously means keeping secrets from parents and setting children against their families with the queered schools playing the role of savior and protector. Ostensibly, those secrets are about sexuality, which is the motte of this particular manipulation. In fact, what is being hidden is that the children are being groomed into the cult of Queer Theory and becoming socially and emotionally locked into supporting Queer Activism. The children are misled to believe their parents will reject *them*, rather than the Queer Activism and grooming, if they find out about this, driving a wedge between parents and

180   ibid.
181   Schmidt, M. (2023, May 17). *Last parent in lawsuit over Madison Schools gender identity guidance drops appeal.* Madison.com. https://madison.com/news/state-regional/government-politics/lawsuit-madison-gender-identity-school/article_22eedc80-1f50-11ee-83fb-fb5b3c27f6cd.html

children in order to destroy families and strengthening ties to the Queer Cult being promoted at the school.

Returning to the AACAP—the association has filed many similar briefings in court battles nationwide. The MMSD's gender affirmation policies are an egregious affront to parental rights, and they aren't at all uncommon in other districts. We'll cover this topic more in the next chapter. For now, it's essential to understand that the AACAP rushed to MMSD's aid successfully because Queer Activists have queered developmental psychology. Developmental psychologists nationwide now push Queer Cult doctrines like the idea that all children are "assigned a sex at birth" and have a "gender identity" that must be affirmed, parents be damned. These beliefs guide and shape their clinical practices and activism. The AACAP defends secretive "gender-affirming" school policies and practices because the AACAP has deemed the *queer approach* to child development as the *only approach* that is "safe" and "effective."

Queer Activists have long claimed that societal stigma causes the significant rates of depression, anxiety, and suicidality observed in "transgender," "gender nonconforming," and "non-binary" youth. Their argument rests on the idea that society is forcing children to "identify with their sex assigned at birth" and assume one of two available "gender" roles. Organizations like the AACAP and the American Psychological Association (APA), informed (read: bullied) by relentless queer activism, have adopted the same arguments. For more than a decade, the AACAP and APA have worked to transition away from traditional models and theories of child development and towards queer developmental psychology—or, as I will call it, Queer Cult Psychology (QCP).

The major shift from classifying *sex confusion* as a psychological abnormality that should be taken seriously and treated accordingly to classifying "gender dysphoria" as a path to "open exploration of a child's gender identity with no goal in sight"[182] happened in 2013. That year, the APA's *Diagnostic and Statistical Manual of Mental Disorders* (DSM-5) was updated to replace "gender identity disorder" with "gender dysphoria." The switch was made because the word "disorder" was considered stigmatizing. Additionally, the "gender dysphoria" diagnosis was moved out of the "sexual disorders" categories and into a category of its own. Most importantly, the DSM-5 shifted away from a focus on *identity* and towards a focus on *distress*.

In previous versions of the DSM, a "gender identity disorder" diagnosis was considered a mental health disorder. The disorder was located in *identity* itself, meaning clinicians should treat a person who identifies with a sex other than their sex in a way that helps them overcome their *identity crisis*. The DSM-5, however, focuses on the psychological distress a person experiences due to a mismatch between their "gender identity" and their "assigned sex." That is, the DSM-5 doesn't consider "gender dysphoria" a mental health disorder or an identity crisis. The DSM-5 doesn't care about the *identity* crisis that people with *sex confusion* experience—it only cares about resolving the *distress* brought on by the crisis. This means that the principal authority for psychiatric diagnoses in the United States directs psychologists to *affirm the chosen identity* of a sex-confused child to relieve the crisis.

DSM not only determines how mental disorders are defined and diagnosed, it also impacts how people see themselves and how we see each other. While diagnostic terms facilitate clinical care and

---

182   Turban, J. L. (2017). Transgender Youth: The Building Evidence Base for Early Social Transition. *Journal of the American Academy of Child and Adolescent Psychiatry*, 56(2), 101–102.

access to insurance coverage that supports mental health, these terms can also have a stigmatizing effect.

DSM-5 aims to avoid stigma and ensure clinical care for individuals who see and feel themselves to be a different gender than their assigned gender. It replaces the diagnostic name "gender identity disorder" with "gender dysphoria," as well as makes other important clarifications in the criteria. It is important to note that gender nonconformity is not in itself a mental disorder. The critical element of gender dysphoria is the presence of clinically significant distress associated with the condition. (American Psychiatric Association, 2013)

The DSM-5 updates undeniably reflected two decades of queer activism in psychology. That activism started really paying off in the late 2000s, as the APA's 2008 declaration *APA Resolves to Play Leading Role in Improving Treatment for Gender-Variant People* demonstrates.[183] The declaration revealed that the APA's governing Council of Representatives adopted a resolution to "support legal and social recognition of transgender individuals consistent with their gender identity and expression," "support… medically *necessary* [emphasis added] treatment for transgender and gender-variant people," "recognize the benefit and *necessity* [emphasis added] of gender transition treatments for appropriately evaluated individuals," and "call on public and private insurers to cover these treatments."[184] Additionally, the declaration revealed that an APA *Task Force on Gender Identity and Gender Variance* had worked for more than two years to review the APA's "transgender" policies. The resulting recommendations

---

183 American Psychological Association. (2008, August 17). *APA resolves to play leading role in improving treatment for gender-variant people* [Press release]. https://www.apa.org/news/press/releases/2008/08/gender-variant
184 ibid.

included developing "separate practice guidelines for transgender clients" and encouraging "more research into gender identity and expression."

The DSM-5 facilitated a tectonic shift in children's developmental psychology. No longer are children considered "abnormal" or "off track" for thinking they were "born in the wrong body." Instead, psychologists work tirelessly to affirm children's feelings, hoping to alleviate and resolve the distress of "gender dysphoria." In practice, this amounts to *affirming a child's mental health disorder*—celebrating it!—rather than helping that child to navigate it in a clinically efficacious manner.

CHILDHOOD INNOCENCE

Beneath all of this, and as a final impediment to Queer Theory, is developmental psychology, particularly childhood developmental psychology. This field has long recognized that growing up is a developmental process containing certain milestones that takes place within boundaries usually defined as "age-appropriate." Sex, sexuality, and even romantic or many emotionally involved relationships are not developmentally appropriate for children and can do lasting psychological damage if introduced irresponsibly. Learning to categorize the world at first concretely—*man, woman, boy, girl*—before moving to more complicated and nuanced understandings of ambiguities and differences is developmentally crucial to developing brains. All of this stands firmly in the way of Queer Theory and its ambitions to queer the child.

Queer Theory colonized and captured developmental psychology by attacking the notion of a *normal and innocent child*. The Queer Theory literature will not let one escape the idea that the ruling class in society (people who own "normalcy" as Bourgeoisie private property) uses the concepts of "normal child" and "childhood innocence" to keep children from exploring their true *queer nature.* In this view, *the normal and innocent child* is a justification for pushing all children through a "cisheterosexual" developmental track.

There is perhaps no better paper to turn to than Hannah Dyer's *Queer futurity and childhood innocence: Beyond the injury of development* to summarize Queer Theory's view of the "normal and innocent child" progressing through a "normal" developmental track. What the weird title of the paper indicates is that believing in and protecting childhood innocence limits the full range of the child's future life in terms of how queer (recall: politically radical) he might be. That is, growing up normal and safeguarded by developmental appropriateness as outlined in rigorous child developmental psychology is characterized as a kind of *injury* to the child! In brief, believing in age-appropriate approaches backed through child developmental psychology allegedly *injures* kids who might otherwise have grown up to be Queer Activists by exposing them to a "normal" childhood that threatens to "straighten" them, against their best interests.

Borrowing from Foucault's idea that the scientific disciplines serve as a regulatory "regime of truth" that perpetuates the status quo, Queer Activists like Dyer argue that psychologists are deeply "implicated in the harming of gay kids."[185] Queer Theory takes developmental psychology to task "for their catastrophic support for beliefs that queer childhood was not viable or healthy."[186] In this view, psychologists have served as a strong arm for the *normal society*, taking "queer children" and "straighten[ing] out their futures."[187] Allowing young children to understand the world in terms of simple, unambiguous, concrete, natural, normal, and

185 Dyer, H. (2016). Queer futurity and childhood innocence: Beyond the injury of development. *Global Studies of Childhood,* 7(3).
186 ibid.
187 ibid.

real categories crucial to their healthy development, categories like *man, woman, boy, girl,* is, from the demented view of Queer Theory, an act of "straightening" kids and stealing from them the possibility of a queer future, thus oppressing them.

According to Queer Activists, what used to be called "gender identity disorder" harmed "queer" children because "as a diagnostic classification [it] assumed the ability to detect impulses not yet organized as queer identity and realign them with heterosexuality."[188] That is, "gender identity disorder" was a way to "fix" children rather than allow them to be "who they really are." And allowing children to be "who they really are" requires ditching old paradigms in favor of "embracing [children's] queer curiosity and patterns of growth."[189] Queer developmental psychology must "address the child as always already queer."[190]

The idea that developmental psychology should abandon traditional theories and practices in favor of *queer possibilities* rests on the idea that society scripts children's futures. Queer Theory claims that *the soul is the prison of the body,* and society convinces children's souls to materialize certain futures on their bodies. That is, Queer Theory argues that disciplines like psychology serve to discipline kids that are stepping out of line, convincing them to get back on a predetermined developmental track, ultimately growing up and *performing* as a straight man or a straight woman. In this view, society treats all kids as "proto-heterosexuals" needing continuous developmental conditioning.

Before Queer Theory colonized the discipline, developmental psychologists worked to help children understand that "It Gets Better."[191] They worked with children to help them constructively

---

188   ibid.
189   ibid.
190   ibid.
191   ibid.

navigate their issues. An "it gets better" approach treats a child's disorders *as disorders* that can be addressed while stressing that things will improve in time. Queer Theory could not tolerate that message because that message doesn't address the here and now as defined on the cult's terms. Queer Activists think that telling kids "it gets better" only stabilizes a definable future within the current sociopolitical order. "It gets better" postpones feelings to the "mythical adulthood," requiring children to tolerate the intolerably oppressive social fabric they are drowning in.

A queer conception of child development is meant to "rupture conventional schemas of 'growing-up,'" as it undoes "anticipated congruency" and "the enforcement of strict borders between childhood and adulthood." Queer Cult Psychology "find[s] pleasure" in tearing down traditional theories of childhood developmental stages and replacing them with queer possibilities. That this is likely to induce crises for the children, as we saw, is considered a queer opportunity. That it will lead to psychological damage and personality disorders is viewed as an oppressive myth used to uphold the "normal" status quo of a cisheteronormative society.

For Queer Activists, the key societal construct that justifies the traditional and alienating [as Marx would use it!] developmental track is "childhood innocence." The Queer Theory literature is unambiguous in this claim. Queer Activists believe that "childhood innocence" is a political construct that normal people use to keep children from learning about their true queer sexuality and desire. The "innocent child" is nothing more than a myth normal people tell society to control what children are exposed to. "Childhood innocence" keeps children away from forbidden knowledge—*away from taking a bite of the apple.* Queer Activists believe they must "queer the rhetoric of innocence that constrains all children and help to refuse attempts to calculate the child's future before it has the opportunity to explore desire."

The Queer Cult does not believe that children are innocent. Queer Activists believe children are full of queer sexuality and desire, claiming that society just suppresses and restricts those instincts to protect a *normal child* and their *normal future.* What they lack is *initiation.* In this view, all children are capable of reason and consent—capable of true human agency, as someone like Paulo Freire would define it. Queer Activists, like Dyer, claim that making childhood sexuality taboo "hurt[s] children's curiosity and imagination" in an effort to protect a child's "assumed proto-heterosexuality."[192] The Queer Cult isn't interested in labeling things as too taboo for children. The Queer Cult is invested in fully ramping up the taboo while "understanding the possibility for children and youth to recruit amounts of bodily pleasure."[193]

> Queer theories of childhood are often brave in the ways that they wade into such taboo territory in order to show how what is considered perverse is often a mode of securing heteronormativity. Queer theory can be helped in its desires to prove that children are capable of possessing complexity and sexuality by exploring work done in the fields of early childhood studies and sociological studies of childhood. This is because these fields and their associated methods of inquiry prioritize the child's possession of knowledge and agentic relation to the world. (Dyer, 2016)

It can't be overstated that Queer Theory thinks all children are sexual. The Queer Cult thinks society has constructed a myth of the "innocent child" to repress children's sexuality so they can't explore and experience it until they are already conditioned

---

192   ibid.
193   ibid.

to be heterosexual or, at the very least, conditioned to fit into and stabilize a heterosexual society. In this sense, society uses the language of childhood sexual trauma to "foreclose careful consideration of the child's agentic relationship to perverse and queer sexuality."[194] Defining children as innocent prevents all children from being exposed to queer forms of sexuality and desire before their future is settled. The "innocent child" has but one path to choose from—cisheterosexuality—as all other queer possibilities are deemed "developmentally inappropriate."

BULLDOZING THE WALL

Hannah Dyer's *Queer futurity and childhood innocence* isn't an outlier in the Queer Theory literature. Queer Activists consider childhood "an arguable crucible or ground zero of all sexual politics."[195] They think this way because they believe children are pawns that normal people use to protect their dominant interests. In this view, who gets to decide what "a child," "childhood," and "innocence" mean determines the future of society. If normal people get to define these concepts, then the future will be normal. If Queer Activists get to define these concepts, then the future will be *queer*. "Queer futurity" is a vision of a future that isn't limited by current societal norms and expectations, particularly those related to sex and sexuality. Hannah Dyer and other Queer Activists make clear that any hope for queer futurity is lost in the concept of "the innocent child," so "the innocent child" is a barrier they know they must destroy. Or, as Queer Activist Lee Edelman says in his book *No Future: Queer Theory and the Death Drive*:

194 ibid.
195 Janssen, D. F. (2012). *Queer theory and childhood*. Oxford Bibliographies.

Fuck the social order and the Child in whose name we're collectively terrorized; fuck Annie; fuck the waif from *Les Mis*; fuck the poor, innocent kid on the Net; fuck Laws both with capital Ls and with small; fuck the whole network of Symbolic relations and the future that serves as its prop.[196] (Edelman, 2004, p. 29)

Queer Activists queered developmental psychology because the discipline was a significant barrier to Queer Cult initiation. In the past, psychologists considered children innocent and incapable of grasping the concepts of sexuality and desire. This was a huge problem for Queer Activists who believed that children *must explore sexuality, gender, and desire* before the clock of "normalcy" strikes midnight. Twenty years ago, it would have been considered child abuse to discuss sexuality and desire with little kids. Likewise, "affirming" a child's mental health disorder would have been considered psychologically abusive. Queer Pedagogy would have been stopped dead in its tracks. Today, all of this is considered developmentally appropriate.

Developmental psychology was the great wall that prevented Queer Activists from presenting, discussing, and encouraging developmentally *inappropriate* ideas, concepts, and themes with kids. The discipline was bulldozed by Queer Activists who endlessly declared that "childhood innocence" creates an unjust distinction between appropriate and inappropriate discussions and content. Queer Theory dissolves distinctions, melding opposites together and creating a *new whole* understood on its own terms. In this case, Queer Activists claimed that what is considered appropriate or inappropriate is arbitrarily defined by those in power for their own benefit. So, nothing is appropriate or inappropriate—everything is contextual and subjective. But, because

---

196 Edelman, L. (2004). *No Future: Queer Theory and the Death Drive*. Duke University Press. (p. 29).

Queer Activists claim to know the truth about how the world works, they think they are the only ones who can determine the correct context of any given situation. Ketanji Brown Jackson felt she couldn't define the word "woman" during her U.S. Supreme Court confirmation hearing because Queer Activists have bullied everyone into thinking that question must be deferred to them. Queer Activists think they are the only ones capable of answering questions related to sex, "gender," and sexuality. Their insight is considered *sacred*, and they say talking to kids about sex, sexuality, and desire is not only appropriate but necessary.

The Queer Cult uses Queer Pedagogy to coerce children to bite *the apple* and learn about the secrets of queer sex, sexuality, and desire. Queer Pedagogy exists to take innocent children and initiate them into the revealed knowledge of the Queer Cult. This initiation process intentionally places kids into an identity crisis. Now, a parent can't take their child to a developmental psychologist to address sex and "gender" confusion because the psychologist serves only to *affirm the initiation*. The only thing waiting for a child with "gender dysphoria" on the other side of the referral is Queer Cult Psychology.

Queer Activists, following Eve Kosofsky Sedwick's seminal work *Epistemology of the Closet*, fundamentally believe that innocence/initiation is a binary that must be overcome. Like the binaries of "appropriate" vs. "inappropriate" and "man" vs. "woman," innocence vs. initiation must be dissolved, revealing a new, higher truth: namely, that innocence is a social construct normal people use to initiate children into cisheterosexuality. In this view, innocence *is* initiation and initiation *is* innocence. Queer Activists think the two concepts are the same if one can only view them from the more elevated state of queer consciousness.

"The closet" is where the magic happens—where innocence and initiation become one and the same. Queer Activists use

Queer Pedagogy to force kids into the closet where they develop their queer consciousness and transcend their innocence *through initiation* into the Queer Cult. The closet, where you keep secrets from others like your parents, is where children are initiated, learning that they aren't so innocent after all—they're *queer*.

Some parents are demanding their day in court after learning that the "inclusive" education their children are receiving is *queer*. When that day arrives, they are met by the expert testimony of a Queer Cult psychologist who is all too thrilled to tell them that their "innocent" child isn't so innocent after all. "If you scratch a child," they might say, "you will find a queer."[197]

---

197 Stockton, K. B. (2009). *The Queer Child, or Growing Sideways in the Twentieth Century*. Duke University Press. (p. 1).

Chapter 8

QUEERING PARENTAL RIGHTS

Queer Activists do not tolerate anything that gets in their way, including parents. If the language games, lies, and covert maneuvers don't work, Queer Activists will not hesitate to attempt to explicitly deny a parent's fundamental right to direct the upbringing and education of their children.

In November of 2021, parents represented by the Wisconsin Institute For Law & Liberty sued the Kettle Moraine School District (KMSD) in Waukesha County, Wisconsin, arguing that the district had violated their constitutionally protected parental rights.[198]

> This action seeks to vindicate one of the most fundamental
> constitutional rights every parent holds dear: the right to raise
> their children. The Kettle Moraine School District has violated

---

198   B. F. & T. F. v. Kettle Moraine School District, No. 21-CV- (Waukesha Cty., Wis. Cir. Ct.).

this foundational right by undermining and overriding parents' decision-making role with respect to a major and controversial issue. Specifically, the District has adopted a policy to allow, facilitate, and "affirm" a minor student's request to transition to a different gender identity at school—without parental consent and even over the parents' objection.[199]

The Wisconsin Institute For Law & Liberty lawsuit outlined a nightmare scenario that parents nationwide are increasingly forced to grapple with. In 2020, a twelve-year-old girl attending KMSD began experiencing "significant anxiety and depression, and also began questioning her gender." Her parents temporarily withdrew her from the school district to allow her to receive professional mental health services. But rather than helping the child work through her anxiety and depression, the medical center "quickly 'affirmed' that she was really a transgender boy and encouraged her to transition to a male identity."[200]

The girl's parents decided that affirming their child's decision and allowing her to "transition" immediately would be against their daughter's best interests. Instead, the parents "wanted their daughter to take time to explore the cause of her feelings before allowing such a significant change to her identity."[201] However, their daughter wanted school staff to adopt her new male name and pronouns when she returned to school. Her parents notified the Kettle Moraine School District to let their daughter's school principal and guidance counselor know that the district should continue to use their daughter's legal name and female pronouns upon her return. The district denied this request, telling the

---

199   ibid.
200   ibid.
201   ibid.

parents that they would use their daughter's preferred name and pronouns when she returned to school.

The parents immediately withdrew their daughter from the school district. They also "cut ties with the mental health center and began searching for therapists that would not rush to 'affirm' an alternate gender identity." Within weeks, their daughter's demeanor changed, and she no longer wanted to "transition" to a male identity. She no longer identified as "transgender," adding that "affirmative care really messed me up."[202]

The parents enrolled their daughter in a new district but quickly realized that their new district also had "gender identity" policies that subverted parental rights. The lawsuit states, "Staff at the new school district told the [redacted] that they also have the same policy as the Kettle Moraine School District, and would follow the same approach if their daughter ever wanted to transition at school again." With nowhere to turn, the parents were forced to take KMSD to court. "Without a judicial decision establishing their constitutional rights as parents," the lawsuit reads, "they may be forced to go through this whole experience again."[203]

Queer Activists have and continue to queer parental rights. They believe it shouldn't be normal for parents to direct their child's upbringing. So, they use policy and gaslighting to circumvent "problematic" parents who don't want schools to manipulate, abuse, and brainwash their children. The Kettle Moraine School District's gender identity policies—which serve to *queer parental rights*—are not uncommon.

According to a 2023 report by The Defense of Freedom Institute for Policy Studies (DFI), nearly half of the nation's largest school districts "allow students to use names and pronouns

---

202 ibid.
203 ibid.

at school aligned with their gender identity without parental knowledge and consent."[204]

> In some of the nation's largest public school districts, it is easier for a student to choose a new name and pronouns than it is to get an aspirin from the school nurse. At least three million K–12 students in 25 districts are given free rein to choose their gender identity at school by changing the name and pronouns used by school employees without parental consent, even though their schools require parental permission to dispense over-the-counter medication to those same children.[205]

Queer Activists groom children into cult identities. The consequences are disastrous, and most parents are unaware of the danger. It's not for lack of attention—the schools are doing everything possible to hide childrens' spiritual awakenings.

HIDING INFORMATION

Schools attempt to justify their radical gender identity policies with a familiar moral argument: revealing a student's "transgender" or "gender non-conforming status" to a parent may place that student in danger. A student's parents might not be happy that their child is gay or transgender, the argument goes, so "outing" a student to their parents could place that student in harm's way. In the most extreme cases, parents might disown their gay or lesbian child.

This argument is used as a moral battering ram to break open parental rights and allow Queer Activists to determine what all

---

204 Moribito, A. (n.d.). *Pills and pronouns: School districts require parental consent for over-the-counter medicine but not new names and pronouns.* Defense of Freedom Institute (DFI). https://dfipolicy.org/wp-content/uploads/2023/02/PillsPronouns_FINAL.pdf
205 ibid.

parents should be allowed to know about their child's schooling. Of course, there are cases where parents might not accept the fact that their child is gay. But gender identity policies have nothing to do with whether or not a child happens to be gay or lesbian. Gender identity policies have everything to do with hiding a student's *gender identity* from parents. "Gender identity" *does not exist outside of Queer Theory*, and gay children *don't have a gender identity*—they just happen to be gay. Said another way, gender identity policies aren't implemented to conceal a child's potential *sexual* preferences. Gender identity policies are designed and implemented to hide what a child is *becoming*. They hide that children are becoming queer, as in they conceal how a child is learning to break away from the idea that sex, sexuality, and gender are stable categories. So, gender identity policies, like this example taken from Montgomery County Public Schools (MCPS) in Maryland, don't protect gay and lesbian kids from unaccepting parents—they serve to hide the *queering of children* from parents.

> Prior to contacting a student's parent/guardian, the principal or identified staff member should speak with the student to ascertain the level of support the student either receives or anticipates receiving from home. In some cases, transgender and gender nonconforming students may not openly express their gender identity at home because of safety concerns or lack of acceptance. Matters of gender identity can be complex and may involve familial conflict. If this is the case, and support is required, Student Welfare and Compliance (SWC) should be contacted. In such cases, staff will support the development of a student-led plan that works toward inclusion of the family, if possible, taking safety concerns into consideration, as well as student privacy, and recognizing that providing support for a student is critical, even when the family is nonsupportive.[206]

---

206 Montgomery County Public Schools. (n.d.). *Guidelines for respecting gender*

Many schools do everything they can to hide the radical politicization of children's minds and bodies from parents, going as far as minimizing the use of permission slips and "other school-specific forms that require disclosure of a student's gender."[207] MCPS explicitly states that "unless the student or parent/guardian has specified otherwise, when contacting the parent/guardian of a transgender student, MCPS school staff members should use the student's legal name and pronoun that correspond to the student's sex assigned at birth."[208]

Queer Activists do not shy away from their intentions. They brag about them. One Queer Activist in the Eau Claire Area School District (ECASD) in Wisconsin posted a flyer in their classroom that reads, "If your parents aren't accepting of your identity, I'm your mom now."[209] Like all ECASD teachers, this teacher had previously received professional development training related to the district's *Administrative Guidance for Gender Identity Support* policy. A recent lawsuit filed against the district revealed that this training included a facilitator's guide that stated, "Remember, parents are not entitled to know their kids' identities. That knowledge must be earned."[210]

The ECASD, like many school districts with gender identity policies, develops specific and actionable "gender support plans" to guide the queering of children. These secret plans allow school staff not only to determine whether or not to hide a student's new name and pronouns from their parents, but also to determine

---

identity. Retrieved January 17, 2023, from https://www.montgomeryschoolsmd .org/uploadedFiles/students/rights/0860.22_GenderIdentityGuidelinesFor Students_WEB.pdf

207   ibid.

208   ibid.

209   Parents Protecting Our Children v. Eau Claire Area School District, No. (W.D. Wis.)

210   ibid.

what types of facilities a child will access while at school. For instance, a school may "affirm" a male student's *female gender identity* by allowing that male student to use the girls' bathroom facilities or locker rooms. The pending lawsuit against the ECASD states:

> The Gender Support Plan identifies the facilities the child can use, including restrooms, locker rooms, facilities for class trips, and lodging for overnight trips. For overnight trips, there is no requirement that anyone notify the parents that their children will be staying in overnight opposite-sex lodging facilities. The only requirement is that appropriate accommodations are made with the lodging facility. There are also sections for extracurricular activities, including who needs to be notified regarding the plan for extracurricular activities, what to do if there are siblings, and how to support the siblings.[211]

Hiding "gender affirmation" plans from parents with "gender non-conforming" or "trans" identifying students *affects all parents*. Take, for instance, an incident on March 3, 2023, in a girls' athletic locker room in Sun Prairie, Wisconsin. After participating in a swim unit for their physical education class, four high school freshman girls—14-year-olds—were joined by an 18-year-old male student in their showers.

> The girls entered the shower area with their swimsuits on, which was their common practice as they rinsed off. As they began to shower, the male student approached them, entered the shower area, announced "I'm trans, by the way," and then undressed fully and showered completely naked right next to one of the girls. He was initially turned towards the wall but eventually turned and fully

---

211   ibid.

exposed his male genitalia to the four girls. Understandably, the girls were caught off guard and shocked, closed their eyes, and tried to hurry up and leave the showers as quickly as possible.[212]

One of the girls involved in the incident told another student about it, and that student informed student services. Rather than reporting the incident to the Sun Prairie Area School District's Title IX coordinator, as required by federal law, school administrators at Sun Prairie East High School reportedly did nothing. It wasn't until the girls' parents involved in the incident became aware that school administrators apologized and "assured parents that the issue had been addressed *with the transgender student*" by referencing a vague *Restroom and Locker Room Accessibility Guidance* policy.[213] As noted by an ongoing lawsuit brought against the Sun Prairie Area School District:

> Under the guidance document, males may still use the girls' locker room and may do so without any regard for the privacy or comfort of female students. The guidance only suggests that if a biological male "makes any request regarding the use of locker rooms," then SPASD administrators will evaluate the request on a "case-by-case basis." What if there is no such request? Is permission to use the girls' locker room required? Who evaluates whether access will be permitted? The policy does not answer these questions. It is quite

212   Wisconsin Institute for Law & Liberty. (2023, April 19). *Re: Serious violation of girls' privacy rights in Sun Prairie East locker room* [Letter to Sun Prairie Area School District Board of Education]. Retrieved from https://will-law.org/wp-content /uploads/2023/04/2023-04-19-Letter-to-SPASD-Board-re-EHS-Locker-Room -Incident-w.-attachme.pdf
213   Wisconsin Institute for Law & Liberty. (2023, April 19). *Re: Serious violation of girls' privacy rights in Sun Prairie East locker room* [Letter to Sun Prairie Area School District Board of Education]. Retrieved from https://will-law.org/wp-content /uploads/2023/04/2023-04-19-Letter-to-SPASD-Board-re-EHS-Locker-Room -Incident-w.-attachme.pdf

telling that, according to the guidance document, if biological girls desire more privacy, it is *the girls* who must leave and use a separate bathroom or locker room. This is precisely backwards.[214]

MEDICAL TRANSITION

Queer Activists groom students into Queer Theory by queering school policies, procedures, classroom norms, and teaching methods. They push kids to deconstruct their identities *critically* until a child no longer knows *who* or *what they are*. Queer Activists then offer gender support plans and social transitioning to the now confused, anxious, and bewildered children as a way out of the manufactured identity crisis. But children are not only encouraged to transition socially. They are also encouraged to transition medically, with devastating consequences.

Queer Theory has captured the U.S. healthcare industry. In 2018, The American Academy of Pediatrics (AAP), which is the largest professional association of pediatricians in the United States, released a policy statement urging support for "gender-affirming approach[es]" titled *Ensuring Comprehensive Care and Support for Transgender and Gender-Diverse Children and Adolescents*.[215] According to the statement, youth who identify as transgender and gender diverse (TGD) should have access to "various interventions" to "better align their gender expression with their underlying identity." These "gender affirmation" interventions include social affirmation, the administration of puberty blockers, cross-sex hormone therapy, and "gender-affirming" surgeries.[216]

The AAP statement embraces some of the most radical claims

214   ibid.
215   Rafferty, J. (2018). Ensuring Comprehensive Care and Support for Transgender and Gender-Diverse Children and Adolescents. *Pediatrics*, 142(4).
216   ibid.

THE QUEERING OF THE AMERICAN CHILD

forwarded by Queer Theory, such as the insistence that "sex" is "an assignment made at birth."[217] The policy, meant to direct and influence clinicians across the country, states that "pediatric primary care providers are in a unique position to routinely inquire about gender development in children and adolescents as part of recommended well-child visits and to be a reliable source of validation, support, and reassurance."[218] By "gender development," the policy isn't referring to *sexual development*, something that a parent would want a qualified and competent pediatrician to monitor in their child. By "gender development," the statement refers to *gender identity development*, something that nearly all parents *do not want* their pediatrician discussing with their child. Likewise, most parents do not want their pediatrician "affirming" or "validating" anything other than their parental rights to refuse such radical psycho-social medical practices.

In late March 2022, five pediatricians who disagreed with the AAP's approach to "gender-affirming" care submitted a resolution calling for a systematic review of evidence and policy related to pediatric gender dysphoria. The resolution, *In Support of a Rigorous Systematic Review of Evidence and Policy Update for Management of Pediatric Gender Dysphoria*, warned that "national health systems and professional health organizations in multiple countries are reconsidering the use of hormones and surgeries as first line treatment."[219] In addition, the resolution called attention to the fact that "puberty blockers followed by cross-sex hormones

---

217   ibid.

218   ibid.

219   American Academy of Pediatrics. (2022, March 31). *In Support of a Rigorous Systematic Review of Evidence and Policy Update for Management of Pediatric Gender Dysphoria*. Retrieved September 6, 2023, from http://web.archive.org /web/20230525012412/https://genspect.org/wp-content/uploads/AAP _Resolution_27_2022.pdf

compromise future fertility and sexual function."[220] To bolster their concerns, the dissenting pediatricians cited several systematic reviews of "gender-affirming" care models in the United Kingdom, Finland, Australia, France, and Sweden. The cited UK review "concluded that the evidence of benefits of puberty blockers and hormonal interventions in youth is inconclusive and that the evidence basis itself is of very low quality." Reaching similar conclusions after a systematic review, the Swedish National Board of Health and Welfare:

> released updated recommendations for gender dysphoria in young people in February 2022, concluding that the risks of hormone treatment for those under 18 outweigh the benefits, and that these interventions should not be offered outside of clinical trials. Sweden's Karolinska Institute's Children's Hospital had already stopped using puberty blockers and cross sex hormones to treat gender dysphoric children outside of clinic trials due to concerns about "low quality evidence" and "extensive and irreversible adverse consequences" in May 2021.[221]

The AAP ignored the dissenting resolution because the concerned pediatricians could not find a sponsor for it. In a blog post supporting the AAP's *Ensuring Comprehensive Care and Support for Transgender and Gender-Diverse Children and Adolescents* statement, AAP president Moira Szilagyi said that "there is strong consensus among the most prominent medical organizations worldwide that evidence-based, gender-affirming care for transgender children and adolescents is medically necessary and appropriate."[222] These "medically necessary" treatments should be

---

220 ibid.
221 ibid.
222 Szilagyi, M. (2022, August 10). *Why We Stand Up for Transgender Children*

administered as early as Tanner stage 2, according to the policy. Girls enter Tanner stage 2 as early as eight years old, while boys enter as early as ten.

The American Psychological Association (APA) also forwards the practice of Queer Theory on children. In a February 2021 *Resolution on Gender Identity Change Efforts*, the APA explicitly states that psychologists must "understand that gender is a non-binary construct that allows for a range of gender identities."[223] The APA also urges psychologists "to help clients in a developmentally appropriate manner to understand the societal contexts of sexism, heterosexism, transphobia, racism and other forms of social oppression, and to use a developmental multicultural- and gender-affirmative framework in research, teaching, training, and supervision."[224]

The APA's *Resolution on Gender Identity Change Efforts* also explicitly states that "invalidation" of "transgender or gender nonbinary identities and diverse gender expressions by others (e.g., families, therapists, school personnel) are forms of discrimination, stigma, and victimization, which result in psychological distress." In other words, the only way to handle a child that says they have adopted a new "gender identity" is to affirm that choice. Any other methods of clinical care—such as helping a child understand their confusion, anxiety, or genuine case of *sex confusion* (what is called gender dysphoria) in a safe and efficacious clinical setting—are tantamount to a "gender identity change effort," which the APA categorizes as "harmful," prejudicial, and discriminatory.

and Teens. Retrieved September 6, 2023, from https://www.aap.org/en/news-room/aap-voices/why-we-stand-up-for-transgender-children-and-teens/

223   American Psychological Association. (2021, February). *Resolution on Gender Identity Change Efforts*. Retrieved September 6, 2023, from https://www.apa.org/about/policy/resolution-gender-identity-change-efforts.pdf

224   ibid.

Gender identity change efforts (GICE) refer to a range of techniques used by mental health professionals and non-professionals with the goal of changing gender identity, gender expression, or associated components of these to be in alignment with gender role behaviors that are stereotypically associated with sex assigned at birth...the APA promotes professional training in gender-affirming practices and opposes professional training in GICE in any stage of the education of psychologists, including graduate training, continuing education, and professional development.[225]

Both the AAP and APA are completely bought into the idea that universal and unquestionable "affirmation" is the *only* way to treat children who have manufactured a new "gender identity" for themselves. Kids are now facing a catastrophic scenario where schools groom them into thinking that they were "born into the wrong body" while the medical establishment waits in the wings, ready to pick up and reconfigure the pieces. In many cases, parents are intentionally kept in the dark.

PUBERTY BLOCKERS, CROSS-SEX HORMONES, AND GENITAL MUTILATION

The risks and complications associated with the dominant "gender-affirming care" model in the United States remain largely hidden from parents. Queer Activists morally bully parents into making hasty, life-altering decisions for their children in the name of "empathy and inclusion." Parents are told that the only way to help "trans" kids be "who they really are" is to pursue dangerous drugs and experimental medical procedures. According to a recent study published in *Archives of Sexual Behavior*, more than half of surveyed parents whose children were referred to a "gender

---

225   ibid.

clinic or specialist" felt pressured "to transition their child socially or medically."[226]

Jamie Reed is a former employee of the Washington University Transgender Center at St. Louis Children's Hospital. Reed describes herself as "a queer woman" who is "politically to the left of Bernie Sanders."[227] In early 2023, Reed turned whistleblower and provided first-hand testimony to the dangers of the radical "gender-affirming care" model that devastates children and their families:

> I personally witnessed Center healthcare providers lie to the public and to parents of patients about the treatment, or lack of treatment, and the effects of treatment provided to children at the Center. I witnessed staff at the Center provide puberty blockers and cross-sex hormones to children without complete informed parental consent and without an appropriate or accurate assessment of the needs of the child. I witnessed children experience shocking injuries from the medication the Center prescribed…Most children who come into the Center were assigned female at birth. Nearly all of them have serious comorbidities including, autism, ADHD, depression, anxiety, PTSD, trauma histories, OCD, and serious eating disorders. Rather than treat these conditions, the doctors prescribe puberty blockers or cross-sex hormones.[228]

In her sworn testimony, Reed also spoke specifically to the medical establishment's use of moral bullying to push parents

---

226   Diaz, S., & Bailey, J. M. (2023). Rapid Onset Gender Dysphoria: Parent Reports on 1655 Possible Cases. *Archives of Sexual Behavior*, 52, 1031–1043.

227   Reed, J. (2023, February 29). I thought I was saving trans kids. The Free Press. https://www.thefp.com/p/i-thought-i-was-saving-trans-kids

228   Reed, J. (2023, February 7). *Affidavit of Jamie Reed*. Retrieved September 6, 2023, from https://ago.mo.gov/docs/default-source/press-releases/2-07-2023 -reed-affidavit—signed.pdf?sfvrsn=6a64d339_2

into consenting to "gender-affirming" treatment plans for their children:

> Doctors at the Center routinely pressured parents into "consenting" by pushing those parents, threatening them, and bullying them. A common tactic was for doctors to tell the parent of a child assigned female at birth, "You can either have a living son or a dead daughter." The clinicians would tell parents of a child assigned male at birth, "You can either have a living daughter or dead son." The clinicians would say this to parents in front of their children. That introduced the idea of suicide to the children. The suicide assertion was also based on false statistics. The clinicians would also malign any parent that was not on board with medicalizing their children. They would speak disparaging of those parents.[229]

Queer Activists argue that puberty blockers are essential components of "gender affirmation" because they "delay" puberty, allowing children more time to think about what "gender" and "sex" they really are. But puberty blockers don't "delay" puberty—they derail it altogether, causing serious injury in the process.

Puberty blockers are incredibly dangerous. They can lead to permanent sterility. This isn't surprising since the class of drugs clinicians use as puberty blockers—GnRH (gonadotropin-releasing hormone) agonists—are also used for chemical castration. They stop boys and girls from producing the hormones their bodies should and need to produce to develop into normal and healthy adults.

According to the FDA, puberty blockers can also lead to increased pressure in the skull "for no obvious reason." According to Mayo Clinic, this pressure includes systems that "mimic those of a brain tumor" and can result in vision loss. Additionally, there

---

229   ibid.

are "reasons to suspect that" puberty blockers "could have negative consequences for neurological development."[230] According
to *Growing Pains*, a groundbreaking report by pediatrician and
endocrinologist Paul Hruz, along with epidemiologist Lawrence
Mayer and psychiatry professor Paul McHugh:

> Though there is very little scientific evidence relating to the effects
> of puberty suppression on children with gender dysphoria — and
> there certainly have been no controlled clinical trials comparing the
> outcomes of puberty suppression to the outcomes of alternative
> therapeutic approaches — there are reasons to suspect that the
> treatments could have negative consequences for neurological
> development. Scientists at the University of Glasgow recently used
> puberty-suppressing treatments on sheep, and found that the spatial
> memory of male sheep was impaired by puberty suppression using
> GnRH analogues, and that adult sheep that were treated with
> GnRH analogues near puberty continued to show signs of impaired
> spatial memory.[231]

Puberty blockers have also been linked to a permanent decrease
in bone density. It's not difficult to find heartbreaking testimony
that details the dangers of pursuing "affirmative" drug treatments
sold to parents as the only way to "save" their child. For example,
Reuters recently reported:

> bone scans indicated that a child, 15 years old at the time, had
> osteoporosis after 15 months on puberty blockers. The teen's
> mother, who asked not to be identified because she works at the

---

230   Hruz, P. W., Mayer, L. S., & McHugh, P. R. (2017, Spring). *Growing Pains: Problems with puberty suppression in treating gender dysphoria.* The New Atlantis. Retrieved September 6, 2023, from https://www.thenewatlantis.com/publications /growing-pains
231   ibid.

hospital where her child was treated, said she thought she had done everything right when her teen came out as a transgender girl. But after the bone scan results…she said she regretted putting her child on puberty blockers. She stopped the Lupron injections and wouldn't agree to hormone therapy.[232]

The medical establishment supports the use of cross-sex hormones as a "medically necessary" measure to push children into "the right body." Cross-sex hormones are generally administered with puberty blockers "to induce something like the process of puberty that would normally occur for members of the opposite sex."[233] For girls, introducing high levels of testosterone leads to the development of "a low voice, facial and body hair growth, and a more masculine body shape." For boys, the introduction of high levels of estrogen results in "breast development and a female-appearing body shape."

Cross-sex hormone treatment is a lifelong commitment and is accompanied by serious risks. According to Mayo Clinic, "feminizing hormone therapy" risks include: blood clots in a deep vein or in the lungs, heart problems, high levels of triglycerides in the blood, high levels of potassium in the blood, infertility, high blood pressure, type 2 diabetes, and stroke.[234] "Masculinizing hormone therapy" risks include: developing male-pattern baldness, sleep

232 Terhune, C., Respaut, R., & Conlin, M. (2022, October 6). *As children line up at gender clinics, families confront many unknowns.* Reuters. Retrieved September 6, 2023, from https://www.reuters.com/investigates/special-report/usa-transyouth-care/
233 Hruz, P. W., Mayer, L. S., & McHugh, P. R. (2017, Spring). *Growing Pains: Problems with puberty suppression in treating gender dysphoria. The New Atlantis.* Retrieved September 6, 2023, from https://www.thenewatlantis.com/publications/growing-pains
234 Mayo Clinic. (n.d.). *Feminizing hormone therapy.* Retrieved September 6, 2023, from https://www.mayoclinic.org/tests-procedures/feminizing-hormone-therapy/about/pac-20385096

apnea, a rise in cholesterol, heart problems, high blood pressure, polycythemia (making too many red blood cells), blood clots in a deep vein or in the lungs, infertility, drying and thinning of the lining of the vagina, pelvic pain, and discomfort in the clitoris.[235]

"Gender-affirmative care" increasingly involves mutilating children's bodies. "Gender-affirming surgeries" often include double mastectomies and phalloplasty for girls "transitioning" into boys. To be clear, a mastectomy, in this context, means cutting off the healthy breasts of girls. A phalloplasty usually involves carving up a girl's forearm to harvest enough skin to create an artificial penis. In boys, vaginoplasty involves inverting the penis to create a fake vagina. Both phalloplasty and vagino-plasty procedures have extremely high complication rates and are often accompanied by a lifetime of medical observation and care.

GENDER-AFFIRMATIVE NATION

The U.S. has witnessed an explosion of children who identify as having a different "gender identity" than the one they were "assigned at birth." More than 300 thousand youth between the ages of 13–17 identify as transgender in the United States.[236] In some areas, nearly 1 in 10 students identify as "gender-diverse."[237]

Fifteen years ago, it would have been difficult to explain what "gender identity" is, let alone find a "gender clinic" on a map. Today, there are "more than 60 comprehensive gender clinics in the United States, along with countless therapists and doctors in

---

235   ibid.

236   Williams Institute. (2022, June). *Transgender Adults in the United States*. Retrieved September 6, 2023, from https://williamsinstitute.law.ucla.edu/publications /trans-adults-united-states/

237   Avery, D. (2021, May 21). *Nearly 1 in 10 teens identify as gender diverse, Pittsburgh study finds*. NBC News. Retrieved September 6, 2023, from https://www.nbcnews .com/nbc-out/out-news/nearly-1-10-teens-identify-gender-diverse-pittsburgh -study-rcna993

private practice," according to the New York Times.[238] Thousands of children are placed on "gender-affirming care" plans each year.

This should concern everyone. The U.S. is now a nation that fast-tracks children into life-altering and dangerous psycho-social medical experiments. Upwards of 80 to 90 percent of "gender dysphoric" youth desist after entering adulthood if no medical intervention is taken.[239] This means that the vast majority of youth flooding into gender clinics today would simply grow up to be normal and healthy (straight, gay, or lesbian) men and women if not for Queer Theory's absolute insistence that these children must be medicalized and treated to "save" them.

Young children cannot consent to what schools and the medical establishment are doing to them. They can't consent to treatments that might render them permanently infertile. They can't consent to drugs that might cause neurological damage, bone loss, or mental health decline. They certainly can't understand how "gender-affirming care" will forever affect their sex lives—many are too young to know what sex is.

Those who "detransition" tell us everything we need to know about our children's "gender-affirming" schools and medical providers. Best-selling author and investigative journalist Abigail Shrier, best known for her book *Irreversible Damage: The Transgender Craze Seducing Our Daughters,* has spoken to more detransitioners than most, and nearly all of them ask the same question—*Where were the adults?*

---

238   Bazelon, E. (2022, June 15). *The Complexities of Transgender Health Care for Kids.* The New York Times. Retrieved September 6, 2023, from https://www.nytimes.com/2022/06/15/magazine/gender-therapy.html
239   Dirks, P. (2020, February 16). Transition as treatment: The best studies show the worst outcomes. The Public Discourse. https://www.thepublicdiscourse.com/2020/02/60143/

THE QUEERING OF THE AMERICAN CHILD

Each of the detransitioners I talked to told a remarkably similar story... Nearly all of the destransitioners I spoke with are plagued with regret. If they were on testosterone for even a few months, they possess a startlingly masculine voice that will not lift. If they were on T for longer, they suffer the embarrassment of having unusual intimate geography—an enlarged clitoris that resembles a small penis. They hate their five-o'clock shadows and body hair. They live with slashes across their chests and masculine nipples... or flaps of skin that don't quite resemble nipples. If they retained their ovaries, once off testosterone, whatever breast tissue they have will swell with fluid when their periods return, often failing to drain properly.... Each of the desisters and detransitioners I talked to reported being 100 percent certain that they were definitely trans—until, suddenly, they weren't. Nearly all of them blame the adults in their lives, especially the medical professionals, for encouraging and facilitating their transitions.[240] (Shrier, 2020, pp. 406–409)

Parents don't know what is happening in their children's schools. They don't know because Queer Activists gaslight and lie to them. If parents are aware of what's happening, that awareness is generally surface-level. The real dangers of "gender-affirmative" care are never given proper consideration. The only thing that matters is "affirming" what a child tells the adult to affirm. Anything else is tantamount to "trans genocide," as Queer Activists often say.

Queer Theory and parental rights are irreconcilable concepts. Parents don't know this when they are told to "use the pronouns." They don't know this when they are told "There is a very likely chance that your child will kill themselves if you don't go along with this." Queer Activists believe the parent/child

---

240   Shrier, A. (2020). *Irreversible Damage: The Transgender Craze Seducing Our Daughters*. Regnery Publishing.

distinction must first be muddled and blurred, then eliminated entirely. They think your kids are their kids.

CONCLUSION

Queer Cult Magic

Indeed, perhaps the most significant way that anti-oppressive teaching is queer is its use of discomfort or crisis. Common definitions of "good" teaching often leave little, if any, room for the moments in education when confronting one's own resistances to disruptive knowledge can be traumatic. In fact, "good" teaching often means that crisis is averted, that lessons are doable and comfortable, that problems are solved, that learning results in feeling better, that knowledge is a good thing...Yet, if anti-oppressive teaching requires disrupting the repetition of comforting knowledges, then students will always need to confront what they desire not to confront. And since learning what we desire not to learn (as when learning that the very ways in which we think, identify, and act are not only partial but also problematic) can be an upsetting process, crisis should be expected in the process of learning, by both the student and the teacher. Like queer activism, queer teaching always *works through* crisis...the goal is to continue teaching and learning through crisis—to continue experiencing the queer.[241] (Kumashiro, 2009, p. 55)

---

241 Kumashiro, K. K. (2009). *Against Common Sense: Teaching and Learning Toward Social Justice* (2nd ed.). Routledge.

American children are *experiencing the queer*. They are in crisis, and a religious cult called Queer Theory put them there. Queer Activists manipulate the energy in their classrooms with queer symbols, signs, and flags. They set the stage for a religious experience where loaded language and cult propaganda flood the room, drowning out thoughts or questions that might challenge queer doctrine. Queer Activists make children fear for their safety and well-being by teaching them to read their world *critically*. They push children to construct new queer political identities to transcend the false reality they've been smashed into. Drag Queens initiate kids into "alternate modes of kinship" so that they may discover their queer consciousness.[242]

The cult of Queer Theory practices their cult religion every day in classrooms nationwide. The evidence is overwhelming, found not only in a ballooning mental health crisis and plummeting reading and math proficiency rates, but also on the material objects of cult witchcraft—children's bodies.

The typical Queer Cultist has no idea that they are in a cult. They reside in the *outer school* and have never studied the works of Michel Foucault, Judith Butler, or Deborah P. Britzman. Likewise, they wouldn't be able to define Queer Theory because they don't even know it exists. An overwhelming majority of Queer Cultists have been so hoodwinked that they have no idea where their beliefs about sex, "gender," and sexuality come from. Most Queer Cultists don't know that much of their daily language is fabricated. For example, no child has a "gender identity" because "gender identity" doesn't exist. "Gender identity" is a queer designer concept manufactured by the cult to coerce people into adopting a cult identity under the promise of fame and

---

242   Keenan, H., & Miss Hot Mess, L. (2021). Drag pedagogy: The playful practice of queer imagination in early childhood. *Childhood Education*, 97(4), 440-461.

salvation. Like most people caught up in cults, they're trapped for social and emotional reasons, not because they've bought into the doctrine. Most want to feel like good people, don't want to be left behind by the progressive march of History they've been led to believe in, don't want to be cut off from their social or professional groups, don't want to be identified as "bad" people (like conservatives), or, perhaps most powerfully, have someone they know or imagine in their lives that they'd be horrified to offend with opinions that disagree with the cult's broad manipulation of society, culture, and individuals.

Queer Activists redefine language without telling you. Specifically, in technical terms, they employ what is known as *conceptual polysemy*, which means that the same word is given more than one meaning. The cult's meaning for the word *always* interprets the concept through critical consciousness and the assumption of pervasive systemic power dynamics. For example, the term "inclusion" in Queer Activism means including Queer Theory, Activism, and Activists and arranging circumstances so they are prioritized and feel centered, which is different than being open to everyone in a way that doesn't account for "power dynamics" like "cisheteronormativity." They then allow people to assume the usual meanings of words (open to all) while intending a specialist cult meaning (queer prioritization to make up for alleged systemic queer exclusion) and, at need, strategically equivocate between the meanings of the words (motte and bailey strategy). By doing this, the *cult's inner school can* communicate with one another in secret while speaking right out in the open. Your typical cult initiate has no clue that words like "inclusion" and "affirmation" mean "exclusion" and "initiation," and no idea that the Queer Theory literature describes "inclusive" and "affirming" spaces in this way:

THE QUEERING OF THE AMERICAN CHILD

inclusion involves inviting people to spaces that are already created, and encouraging them to find a place within an already existing structure...we must become co-conspirators rather than allies, and seek to co-create spaces that are radically different and transformative.

As such, I have chosen to focus on creating spaces that... recognize, honor, and actively celebrate all identities and intersections. The reality of these identities, of these lives, of these experiences, is intimately woven into the very fabric of the space, the ritual format, and the magick and ritual performed.[243] (Harper, 2018, pp. 65–76)

The typical teacher or administrator is initiated into the cult of Queer Theory during her studies at university. There, she learns that society is designed to be unfair and the educator's job is to join her students in *reading the word to change the world*. The cult teaches her that she must celebrate and practice "diversity, equity, and inclusion" to give each of her future students an equal shot at the same outcome. She learns that no one accepts children for who they *really* are, even their parents. She enters the classroom thinking that she has learned the best way to teach children how to read and write, not knowing that all of her training is meant to push her to teach children to "read and write as part of the process of becoming conscious of one's experience as historically constructed within specific power relations."[244] Or, put more simply, her training pushes her to teach children to be Marxists.

The brainwashed among us mostly have no idea that all of

243   Harper, S. (2018). For thou art goddess: Creating affirmative goddess community. In L. Harrington & T. F. Kulystin (Eds.), *Queer Magic: Power Beyond Boundaries* (pp. 65–76). Mystic Productions Press.
244   Shor, I. (2009). What is critical literacy? In A. Darder, M. P. Baltodano, & R. D. Torres (Eds.), *The critical pedagogy reader* (2nd ed., pp. 282–304). Routledge. (p. 282).

the ritual and magic of "empathy" and "inclusion" sometimes leads to medical professionals poisoning children with drugs typically used to castrate sex predators. Your everyday, run-of-the-mill Queer Cultist has no idea that butchers are taking scalpels to kids—no idea that this butchery is justified by a belief that children can *trans*cend "being born in the wrong body."

Queer Cult magic is strong. Queer Activists concocted their spells in the centuries-old cauldron of Romantic Idealism and eventually Marxism, where the spells picked up flavors of Gramsci, The Frankfurt School, Marcuse, Foucault, and Freire. In this cauldron, Queer Activists combined a religious revolutionary theory of History with a *queer* revolutionary theory of sex, "gender," and sexuality. Through alchemy, they attempted to turn lead into gold. That is to say; they attempted to create a new series of spells by combining the failed magic of Marxism with the promising magic of postmodern identity politics, transforming both into something considerably more destructive. These spells are seasoned for cultural revolution, hidden in the words and rituals educators everywhere use and practice today. They lead children to bathe in the poisonous brew.

Queer Theory has captured the entire medical establishment. America's *queer* doctors, psychologists, and psychotherapists are witnessing an explosion of sick kids entering their practices. These medical professionals don't know these kids have been poisoned, and because of this, they aren't treating the children they are seeing properly. Many "trans" children enter their first therapy session with a case of queer consciousness, not gender dysphoria. Many kids that walk through the door would otherwise be considered normal and healthy in mind and body had queer activism not poisoned them. Many others are often autistic and have suffered enormous amounts of emotional and physical trauma. The queer therapist doesn't really address any of that—they only see an *awakened soul* that wants to transform their body to reflect their "true self."

Reporting for *City Journal,* Christopher Rufo details how a physician who works in a major children's hospital "has witnessed firsthand how transgender ideology has captured the medical profession and jeopardized the first commandment of the healing sciences: do no harm."[245] When asked, "What do you predict for the future of transgender medicine? Will it continue to gain ground, or will it all fall apart?" the physician, speaking on condition of anonymity, had this to say:

> I don't know. I pray that there is a change. One of the things I've been thinking about is what puberty blockers do to children. This medication is called a "gonadotropin releasing hormone agonist" and it comes in the form of monthly injections or an implant. And because it simulates the activity of this hormone, it shuts down the activity of the hypothalamus. The hypothalamus is this almond-sized structure in your brain, it's one of the most primal structures we have, and it controls all the other hormonal structures in your body—your sexual development, your emotions, your fight-or-flight response, everything. But it shouldn't be described in such cold physiological terms because your hypothalamus is not just a hormone factory. It's this system that allows you to stand in awe of the beauty of a sunset, or to hear the sounds of orchestral music and to stop whatever you're doing and want to listen. And I always think that if someone were to ask me, Where is it that you would look for the divine spark in each individual? I would say that it would be somewhere "beneath the inner chamber," which is the Greek

---

245   Rufo, C. F. (2023). *Thrown to the wolves.* City Journal. https://www.city-journal.org/article/transgender-ideology-and-the-corruption-of-medicine

derivation of the term hypothalamus. To shut down that system is to shut down what makes us human.[246]

CULTURAL REVOLUTION

All children poisoned by Queer Theory fight to *abolish normalcy*. Queer Theory exists to blur all boundaries and destroy all norms. Anything considered normal must go. The goal is to capture all of society and dissolve all rules, standards, and categories. It has no limiting principles because it opposes limiting principles *on principle*. Queer Theory is the most acidic concept to ever escape from the academy, and children are learning to play with the acid in their schools. They're also encouraged to take it home and play with it at the dinner table, their social circles, and communities. Whether they know they are doing it or not, teachers nationwide are teaching kids to be abnormal, deviant, unpredictable, and wholly destructive.

Queer Theory teaches kids that life itself is a prison. Children see illegitimate power everywhere and are trained to pour acid on anyone or anything that tells them "No." The *cult's inner circle* knows that the *Rainbow Guards* are the quintessential lever of cultural revolution. The inner circle knows this because they learned how cultural revolutions work from Chairman Mao Zedong.

You might not know a lot about Mao. That, I would argue, is no accident. Marxists have been in charge of U.S. education for decades, and they've used their position to *redwash* our history. Mao was the chairman of the Chinese Communist Party, founder of the People's Republic of China (PRC), and the poster boy of the New Left in the 1960s. As we now know, the New Left became the Academic Left that now runs our schools. You

---

246   ibid.

can still hear the infamous 1960s chant "Marx, Mao, Marcuse!" echo through college campuses today.

In 1966, Mao launched the Cultural Revolution in China. He used education as *the* lever for prying open the door to totalitarianism. Mao wanted to eliminate all communist party leaders who could challenge him and to regain his power as Chairman, and he used young adults and children to accomplish his objectives.

On 18 August 1966 an extraordinary event took place in Beijing. Over a million people, the majority of them in their teens or early twenties, packed into Tiananmen Square. Waving their Little Red Books, they screamed themselves hoarse in an impassioned outpouring of veneration for their idol, Chairman Mao. This massive demonstration was the first event in the Cultural Revolution, a movement that aimed at nothing less than the creation of a new type of Chinese society and which was to convulse the whole of China for the next decade. Mao had enlisted the youth of China as his instrument for reimposing his will upon the nation and reshaping it according to his vision.

Mao identified 'four olds' as targets for the young to attack – old culture, old thoughts, old customs and old habits… As 'Red Guards', they rushed to do [Mao's] bidding with a terrifying intensity and ferocity. It is doubtful whether any other society has witnessed organized upheaval on such a scale. Hardly anywhere in China, even the remotest regions, remained untouched. There was scarcely a family unaffected by what happened. Millions died; many more millions had their lives irreparably damaged.[247] (China Under Mao: The Cultural Revolution, 1966–76)

---

247   Lynch, M. (n.d.). *China Under Mao: The Cultural Revolution, 1966 - 76.* Retrieved from https://nisis.weebly.com/uploads/1/0/2/9/10295486/lynch_-_effects_of_cr.pdf

Mao understood well that children wish to conform to the standards of their peers. He wielded the youth's desire for "inclusion" and "belonging" to brainwash millions of children into his cult. "From the first day of my schooling, at seven years old, I learned 'I love you Chairman Mao', not 'I love you Mamma or Papa',"[248] recalls a student who attended Mao's schools. "I was brainwashed for eight years and looking back I realise that the Party was doing everything to keep us pure, purifying us so we would live for Mao's idealism, Mao's power."[249]

Mao's Red Guards "felt that [they] were defending China's revolution and liberating the world,"[250] to quote a former member. They believed chaos was more virtuous than order, and the desire for revolution freed them from their previously held moral restrictions.[251] The Red Guards destroyed temples, shrines, monuments, and works of art—anything that represented the tradition of the "old" and "traditional" China. Children insulted, abused, and assaulted their teachers, parents, and grandparents. Anyone deemed insufficiently socialist was targeted for thought reform, where psychological torture methods coerced fake confessions for fabricated crimes. These "struggle sessions" destroyed a person's soul and replaced it with "socialist discipline." In Mao's China, every man, woman, and child was required to have the correct political opinions. Everyone was expected to "do the work" of studying the theory and practice of Marxism. To refuse this was to be treated as an animal without a soul. In Mao's own words:

248 ibid.
249 ibid.
250 ibid.
251 ibid.

Both students and intellectuals should study hard. In addition to the study of their specialized subjects, they must make progress both ideologically and politically, which means that they should study Marxism, current events and politics. *Not to have a correct political point of view is like having no soul* [emphasis added]. (Mao, On the Correct Handling of Contradictions Among the People (February 27, 1957); 1ˢᵗ pocket ed., pp. 43–44)

Mao's Red Guards accomplished their objectives, particularly struggling and deposing Mao's rival Liu Shaoqi, but they became so radical in their cult worship of Mao and his "Marxism-Leninism with Chinese characteristics" that they sent China into an economic and humanitarian crisis. Radicalism is great for destabilizing a society so you can eliminate your enemies and take total control. However, radicalism is terrible for stabilizing your new regime. Mao knew this, so within months of regaining power he turned his People's Liberation Army (PLA) on the Red Guards, forcing an estimated twelve million children and young adults (conservative estimate) out of the cities and into the countryside, where they faced hard labor, malnutrition, and death.[252] Those who refused were brutally murdered. Many were so deeply brainwashed that they went not just willingly but eagerly, chanting about how it would make their brains even more "red."

Although the content of Queer Theory's cultural revolution may differ from Mao's, the methods are the same. Queer Activists are brainwashing children to overthrow our existing society so it can be replaced with a new society. These children harass and abuse any person or idea that gets in their way. They demand new speech codes, affirmations, and special privileges. They think anyone who isn't in their religious cult is an animal without a soul. Anyone who doesn't universally support their

---

252   ibid.

divine wisdom is labeled a far-right conservative bigot. In the end, everyone who doesn't bend the knee is conserving the status quo and must be dealt with accordingly.

Of course, the kids who are all too idealistic will be dealt with once the new (ab)normal is established. I'm not saying children will be carted off into the countryside or sent to awful places to mine cobalt for batteries, but revolutionaries will be violently suppressed in speech and action. The youth groups and organizations that are most aggressive and efficient will be considered "counter-revolutionaries" when the time comes, just like Mao's Red Guards. In an instant, all the love bombing, affirmation, and special privileges will end. When the time comes, the Rainbow Guard will be treated like everyone else, suffering under new and more brutal definitions, categories, and regulations. The cult's inner circle doesn't care about the child who has destroyed their mind and body. Just like Mao, the inner circle only cares about securing the power to mold the world in its image.

THE ANTIDOTE

> Antidotes are agents that negate the effect of a poison or toxin. Antidotes mediate its effect either by preventing the absorption of the toxin, by binding and neutralizing the poison, antagonizing its end-organ effect, or by inhibition of conversion of the toxin to more toxic metabolites. (National Institutes of Health)

We can learn a lot about how to protect our children from the cult of Queer Theory by studying the history of other religious cults, like The People's Temple (Jim Jones), The Branch Davidians (David Koresh), Heaven's Gate (Marshall Applewhite and Bonnie Nettles), The Manson Family (Charles Manson), and Aum

Shinrikyo (Shoko Asahara). Cults aren't new. We understand how they work.

Every cult practices extreme prejudice in shutting down anyone who would question or criticize cult doctrine or practice. So, we must constantly question and criticize our teachers and school administrators when they implement any policies or procedures rooted in Queer Theory. To do this, we must study Queer Theory and use discernment to determine whether or not a policy or procedure aligns with queer religious doctrine. We must study other parents' battles in their districts, learning as much as we can about cult maneuvers and tactics. Work to expose manipulation, language games, and deception. Share what you learn with others.

Every cult pressures members to cut off contact with their family, friends, or anyone who doesn't share their cult beliefs and faith. So, we must work to make our relationships with our children iron-clad. This is the responsibility of every parent. Remember, the cult thinks you—the parent—are in a cult. Queer Activists think your family is part of the cult of *cisheteronormativity and normalcy*. They believe they are saving your child *from you*. Don't make the cult's job easy—do everything you can to create an exceptional relationship with your children and encourage family values.

One can't understand how Queer activists view the relationship between parent and child without first understanding that Queer Theory is Queer Marxism. We spent a solid portion of this book laying out that case for this very moment. For Marxists, the key to unlocking communism is abolishing private property. Queer Theory thinks that *normalcy* is the private property it must abolish, and it finds normalcy *in the relationship between child and parent*. Put simply, Queer Theory works to abolish your relationship with your child. This is why teachers, teachers' unions, and even the

POTUS think that they know what's best for your children—that *your children are their children.*[253] [254] Queer Activists, like the "vulgar" Marxists before them, want to use the State to administer all former privately held property. Queer activists couldn't be more apparent that this is how they think. For instance, take this example from the piece *Children Are Not Property: The idea that underlies the right-wing campaign for "parents' rights"*:

> Like any piece of property, a child has value to conservative activists. They are key to a future the conservative wants to win. Parental rights are merely one path to the total capture of state power and the imposition of an authoritarian hierarchy on us all...In this perspective, rights aren't innate. They're determined instead by a person's place in the conservative hierarchy. The opposite view — that everyone has rights by virtue of their humanity — requires us to change the way we commonly think of children. Liberals aren't immune to the belief that children are property. The mainstream fearmongering over trans youth tells us that much. Yet combating the power of the parental rights movement requires an answering conviction in the rights of children. We can see them as people: uniquely vulnerable, yes, but nevertheless people who have independent minds and will develop private lives of their own.[255]

253 Schemmel, A. (2022, November 14). *Teachers union blasted for insisting educators 'know what students need better than anyone'.* WPDE. Retrieved from https://wpde.com/news/nation-world/teachers-union-blasted-for-insisting-educators-know-what-students-need-better-than-anyone-national-education-association-betsy-devos-nea

254 Jacques, I. (2023, April 27). *Who knows what's best for kids? Hint: Biden and Democrats don't think it's parents.* USA Today. Retrieved from https://www.usatoday.com/story/opinion/columnist/2023/04/27/biden-government-dictate-kids-education-schools-not-parents/11743676002/

255 Jones, S. (2023, April). *Children Are Not Property.* New York Magazine. Retrieved from https://nymag.com/intelligencer/2023/04/children-are-not-property.html

The goal of isolating children from their parents is to make it easier to expose them to constant propaganda and indoctrination. Parents, knowing this is how cults operate, must identify the actors that are isolating their children and use every peaceful and legal means necessary to remove them from power. Your children are *your children*. They do not belong to the State. Moms for Liberty, the national organization of *joyful warriors* fighting tooth-and-nail to stand up for parental rights at all levels of government, says it best: *We do not co-parent with the government.*

Parents must reintroduce their children to the normalcy of reality, untethered from cult control, cutting out and exposing any queer propaganda for what it is—poison. This is no easy task. The queer education children receive is reinforced by the queer propaganda that finds its way onto their televisions, computers, tablets, and phones. When your child is exposed to queer propaganda it is incumbent on you as the parent to expose that propaganda. There is no template for this, and every family will choose different strategies. I suggest teaching your children how to spot the propaganda themselves. I also suggest heavy doses of mockery and laughter. The regime hates mockery and laughter, and it makes a lot of mistakes when it's upset that people aren't taking it seriously anymore.

Of course, all cults threaten dissenting members with a loss of salvation. So, whether we have our own faith or not, we must explain to our children that the cult offers only a road to hell. Practicing Queer Theory is a sure-fire way to destabilize your life. That is the explicit goal. People who hate their society, family, and existence are easy to manipulate and control. Queer Activists want a critical mass of unstable people so they can wield them like a sledgehammer against the status quo. So, offer children alternatives—your values, beliefs, and judgments. Let them know that, as Americans, they can build whatever life they want to build, but they must set out on the journey by first construct-ing a stable foundation.

Surround your children with people who aren't cultists. Show kids how great *normal* feels. Help your children find and build upon their identity as individuals, not collectivists. Use your dis-cernment when your child seems off. If you feel there is a need to seek professional therapy or medical treatment for any reason, do everything you can to find a provider who isn't a cultist. They are out there, and I suspect the market is experiencing rapid expansion.

Parents—and the parental rights enshrined in the U.S. Constitution—are the antidote to queer poison. Work to negate Queer Theory by binding yourself to it and neutralizing it when it enters your child's life. Know what's going on in your child's classroom. Figure out what your kids think about their own lives. Keep a close eye on what they are exposed to on their phones and computers. *Protect them from the cult.*

YOU HAVE THE ANSWERS

At the outset of this book, we asked the following question:

What would you do if you thought your children were skipping school to join a religious cult?

Maybe you've reached this point and think there is nothing wrong with anything we've covered in this book. Queer Activists certainly wouldn't think there is much wrong with what we've covered—we've spent page after page citing their works and words. We recommend you take some time to review the references we've noted. Very few of the books we've read and cited while conducting our research was critical (we hope, by this point, this word has become a red flag—but in this case, it means what you think it means) of Queer Theory. Nearly all of the citations at the end of *The Queering of the American Child* are sources *in favor* of queering education to queer children to queer all of society. We encourage you to read the books we have cited on these pages. The authors of these books brag about their religious projects. They spend thousands and thousands of pages explaining precisely what they think, why they think it, what they are doing, and what they want to accomplish. All we have done is read those books and believed the authors. We take them at their word because they take their words very seriously. They think language is *everything* because their sacred books tell them that language is more real than the real world. For the Queer Activist, there is no reality outside of the magic of language. They only have their words, and we've done my best to wield those words against them.

In *The Queering of the American Child* we've shared what Queer Theory is, what it's doing in education, how it got there, and what it hopes to accomplish. We wrote this book to join others in signaling the alarm. A Queer Activist might read this book and think, "We've accomplished so much. Keep going. Do the work!" We hope more instead read this book and think, "Am I in a cult? I shouldn't be in a cult."

In answering my question—*What would you do if you thought your children were skipping school to join a religious cult?*—some parents may pull their kids from their public or private schools. That's a great idea. Some parents might schedule parent-teacher conferences to discuss what's happening in their child's class-room. That's a great idea, too. Some parents will join groups like Moms For Liberty, some will have important conversations with their children, some will attend lectures about the state of educa-tion, and some will do nothing. We support all of that. We don't have a lot of prescriptions because we don't know what it is that you can do. What can you do differently now that you know what you know? Only you have the answers to that question.

We do think that we need to recognize Queer Theory for what it is—a religious cult. As a religious cult, Queer Theory has no place in public schools. The First Amendment of the U.S. Constitution states:

> Congress shall make no law respecting an establishment of religion, or prohibiting the free exercise thereof; or abridging the freedom of speech, or of the press; or the right of the people peaceably to assemble, and to petition the Government for a redress of grievances.

Queer Theory clearly violates the Establishment Clause of the First Amendment. Our schools endorse and promote Queer Theory with extreme prejudice. Many of our public officials and professionals are Queer Activists, and they *practice* Queer Theory by creating queer speech codes, policies, procedures, and practices. They use Queer Pedagogy to work to convert children into the Queer Cult. Queer Activists also violate the Free Exercise Clause by excluding any belief, attitude, or behavior that challenges their doctrine. Our children attend public religious institutions, and that case can and must be made. If Queer Theory is recognized as the cult religion it is, then we can remove it from all schools receiving public funds. Doing so would be a monumental victory.

We also think teachers need to start taking a stand. Many educators we talk to have no idea that their classroom practices are a form of religious cult grooming. These teachers think they are "just being empathetic." They are good, decent people who themselves have been brainwashed. Some teachers are speaking out. We need thousands more to join the fight, expose what they are being asked to do with children, and speak out against the *queering* of American children. For the ambitious among you, *Teachers for Liberty* has a nice ring to it.

We're facing an uphill battle. But there is hope. Every day the cult of Queer Theory faces more exposure. The cult's insane policies and practices spark a lot of attention, and parents nationwide are looking hard at their children's education. Some of those parents are taking action, and some are winning. Take, for instance, the mother and daughter who recently sued the Spreckels Union School District in California. According to the lawsuit, the Buena Vista Middle School socially transitioned an 11-year-old girl secretly. The legal team representing the mother and daughter, The Center for American Liberty, said that the girl's school "fostered her identification as a boy, gave her articles on how to conceal her new gender identity from her family, and put her on a 'Gender Support Plan' that instructed school staff to refer to her by a male name and male pronouns." The lawsuit was recently settled and the mother and daughter were awarded $100,000. We need many, many more lawsuits. The message must be clear—"parents will not stand idly by as schools trample on their right to raise their children."[256]

We have been studying Queer Theory for years. We have felt that Americans faced a losing battle for most of that time. We don't feel that way anymore. Queer Theory wasn't on anyone's radar a decade ago. Today, thousands of parents know what it is and are working to expose, reject, and remove it from schools.

In the end, the cult always self-implodes. We can accelerate that process with discernment, exposure, and the rule of law. Remove it from schools, kicking and screaming. That's what a healthy, *normal* society would do.

---

256   Center for American Liberty. (2023, August 29). *Victory! School district held accountable for socially transitioning child behind parent's back.* https://libertycenter.org/victory-school-district-held-accountable-for-socially-transitioning-child-behind-parents-back/

AFTERWORD

by James Lindsay

American education is in the grip of a religious cult. That simple sentence opens this admirable work by Logan Lancing, and it is such a strong and important statement of fact that I have chosen to write an afterword rather than a foreword for this book so that it can be the first statement the reader encounters. That's a stark truth, and it has to be reckoned with. You will have discovered that sentence is completely and undeniably true in these pages. Queer Theory is the doctrine of a religious cult. That cult is Queer Marxism. It seeks societal transformation through the psychosexual transformation of our children. This cult and its influence on children cannot be borne, and they must be borne no longer.

Queer Theory, as the doctrinal engine of the Queer Marxism cult, is ultimately one peculiar manifestation of the Gnostic and Hermetic cults alluded to throughout this text. It's a lot to explain these cults properly here, along with how they became Marxism and eventually Queer Theory, so a short explanation will have to do.

In the briefest expression, Gnostic cults, in any of their forms, are ones that view Being itself, all of material existence including our own lives, as a prison that incarcerates our true spiritual selves, from which we are alienated. Knowing this to be the true nature of reality and ourselves is, for these cults, a hidden and sacred knowledge that enables salvation: liberation from the prison and true reunification with God, the Absolute. Knowing the true nature of reality isn't the key aspect of these cults of secret, hidden, saving knowledge. The secret, hidden, cult knowledge, called "gnosis," which is Greek for knowledge, is always secret, hidden, cult knowledge about *ourselves* and our true nature, as opposed to our false nature we perceive in the fallen, incarcerated world. For the ancient Gnostics, we're spiritual beings, and the material world we inhabit, including our bodies, is profane. It—and the demonic being who created it, called the Demiurge—misleads us into believing we too are matter or, at least, have a material component from which we must escape. No matter how we skew it, Gnostic cults therefore must be skeptical and destructive of reality.

Hermetic cults, by contrast, are similar but built around the idea of transformation. They believe the world as we perceive it is an illusion that obscures the true nature of everything, including ourselves. Transformation in these cults is achieved by seeing through false dualities: where things appear to be different, they are really the same—when understood from a more "enlightened" perspective that is accessed through cult belief and practice. The practice of these cults is *alchemical*. They seek to transform the mundane into the divine through esoteric practices that can liberate the true spiritual aspects of being from the mundane and fallen material aspects. Since all spirit is the One Spirit, and all things are ultimately this Spirit, all distinctions are illusions to be overcome. The mundane, fallen world and we within it must overcome our separateness and return to atonement, sometimes spelled "at-one-ment," with the All.

Though these two prototypical cult structures are different, Marxism and Queer Marxism are *both of them at the same time.*

The two main esoteric cult beliefs are synthesized into one. Their fusion largely took place through what might be considered the New Age movement of the Medieval Period, especially in Europe during the Renaissance. Mystics drew from these ideas as they arrived in Europe from various sources, including ancient writings, importation from India, and fraud. They mixed these ideas and infused them into European systems, including Christianity, and then as the Modern Era dawned, some located their alleged spiritual power not in transcendence but in the social world of civil society. Marxism is the most iconic and destructive result of this evolution of evil.

Though we're referring to Marxism in these cult terms, Karl Marx, for all he did to advance this cult perspective into a global religious phenomenon, does not deserve the credit for hammering the Gnostic and Hermetic cult structures together or for making them palatable for a post-Enlightenment, Western audience. Credit for that feat lies primarily with two of his intellectual predecessors, the French father of Romanticism, Jean-Jacques Rousseau, and the German speculative idealist, G.W.F. Hegel.

Rousseau was undoubtedly a Gnostic. "Man is born free, but everywhere he is in chains," is not only his most famous utterance but also the prototypical Gnostic sentiment. Rousseau didn't look around at the world he was in and feel incarcerated by *Being itself*, in a spiritual sense, however, as did the ancient Gnostics and occultists before him. He felt imprisoned by *social expectations*, specifically the social expectations of being a bourgeois citizen, a city-dweller—what the Germans of the day called a *bürger*. Rousseau, in an important way, relocated the spiritual dimension of human existence, which is incarcerated by the evil Demiurge of Gnostic belief, *within social life*. The expectations of civilized living, that is, society, incarcerate man and prevent him from living whatever life he would. Though it may be impertinent to speculate as to why Rousseau thought this way, his rather famously licentious and extravagant lifestyle, and seemingly permanent allergy to consequences for his actions, may explain it.

To justify his ideas, Rousseau put elevated attention on the Noble Savages of the "uncivilized" world and longed for their fully immediate, sincere lives. The trouble is, he also liked the rather decadent benefits of the city, which he was known to enjoy more than a little. In romanticizing that tension, Rousseau was also a Hermeticist. He sought to find a way to actualize humanity as it *should* be, by transforming us all into "savages made to inhabit cities." That, ultimately, is the poisonous basis for the (Left) Romantic Reaction against the Enlightenment within which Marxism arises. It is also where Gnosticism and Hermeticism as esoteric cult religions began to be fused and tucked away into the societal aspects of life, giving birth to a kind of Sociological Gnosticism.

Marx didn't receive Rousseau's alchemical fantasies about Man reenvisioned as "savages made to inhabit cities" directly. He got those ideas, and the systematic philosophy he operationalized, from Hegel. Hegel, for his own part, was a fan of Rousseau, as was his intellectual predecessor Immanuel Kant and his mystical-intellectual older brother Friedrich Schiller. Hegel adopted the dialectical thought of Kant and Schiller's enthusiasm about the Hermetic transformation of civilized man into "savages made to inhabit cities," which he identified with the word *aufheben*, an odd German word that means to abolish, to keep, and to lift up to a higher level all at the same time. These he combined with the blatant Hermetic mysticism of Jakob Böhme, whom Hegel considered to be Germany's greatest philosopher, perhaps apart from Goethe, who trafficked in the same esoteric currents, all steeped in a unique (Swabian) pietist heresy of Lutheran Christianity that was en vogue at the seminary, the Stift in Tübingen, where Hegel studied and taught. The thing is, like Hegel, Böhme wasn't a philosopher at all, or even theologians. Both were theosophists, which is to say wizards.

The result of Hegel's labor was a systematic "speculative idealist" philosophy that reformulated the Christian Trinity as an unfolding dialectical process of "becoming" in which the Ideal (God, as Father) manifests in Nature and the State (as Son) that carries a *Geist* (Spirit) of society that is, in effect, the Sociological Gnosticism characteristic of Rousseau's Romanticism. His most famous work was dedicated to outlining the workings of this "Spirit," his 1807 *Phenomenology of Spirit*, which he referred to as a "system of science," meant in the mystery-cult Platonic sense he stole from heavily.

Ultimately, this means Hegel was a heretical, cult theologian who outlined a Social-Spiritual idealist cult doctrine based on the idea that God *becomes God* through the philosophical ideas of Man reaching Absolute harmony. His theology posits God as the Absolute Idea, which is the ultimate reconciliation of the Subjective and Objective. Even with the short description given above, this is obviously a Hermetic project that seeks to remove the distinction between the two domains and frame them as two parts of a single whole that can be comprehended on its own. For Hegel, the Subject works on the Object and changes it. As a result, the Subject can thus see himself in the Object he created or transformed, so the Subject is necessarily part of the Object and can know himself to be that. Meanwhile, he can *speculate on the ideal* form of the Object (the Object in itself) upon which he works (thus, "speculative idealist") and engage in further transformations that bring the Object more in line with the Ideal, seeing himself in the process as the Subject who can immanentize the Ideal (in his imagination, a Romantic notion) in reality (the

Object). When these are fully harmonized in all regards and all Objects are made through reflective Subjects into the Ideal, all is Ideal and just a manifestation of the Absolute Idea, or God, and the Subjects who did this work can see themselves to be exactly that. How else could the Ideal be made Object but through the labor of God, which, for Hegel, is to say "philosophers"?

Confusing details aside, all this is to say that Hegel was a Hermetic theosophist using Lutheran motifs in esoteric ways and calling it a "science." God isn't an eternal being in three parts who knows himself to be what he is—"I am what I am." God has to realize what He is before He is truly God. That is, He must *become* God through the dialectical process of removing distinctions (read: clarity) as outlined above. God is the Absolute that doesn't know He is Absolute and therefore has to *become* Absolute through His Creation, the thinking part of which is Man. He Absolutizes at the "End of History," when lives "the Last Man," when the dialectical process concludes with the final reunification of Subject and Object. In other words, this is profound heresy. It's also the hidden and manipulative religious current that has run through the West almost entirely unnoticed, while hiding in plain sight, for almost three centuries.

The "science" Hegel believed himself to be describing is the science of History itself. The project of relentless transformation through dialectical *aufheben*, brought on by bringing opposing factions into conflict and driving that conflict to a resolution through a historical protagonist called a Man of Destiny, is History itself. Hegel believed himself to be outlining the science of how it develops. The (current) Idea is held in the mind of Men who actualize it through the State which gives rise to a society and its *Geist* which eventually moves men to conflict and rupture from which a new, higher Idea is born. For this reason, Hegel venerated the State, accorded it with divine status, and said it was "the Divine Idea as it exists on Earth." The State, led by Men of Destiny, is the mover of History itself.

Karl Marx adopted this philosophy and applied to it the "ruthless criticism of all that exists," which he adapted from a line by the character Mephistopheles (the emissary or voice of Satan) in Goethe's famous rendition of *Faust*. "All that exists deserves to perish," announced Mephistopheles in the drama, and Marx took this as a cue to reformulate Hegel's dialectical system through criticism. Put otherwise, by nominally rejecting Hegel's Christian-ish idealism while retaining his entire esoteric theology otherwise, Marx retooled his program into a wholly negative, or apophatic, theology. The Ideal isn't real or even something men can know because it's just a reflection of what we wish the world was. We can't know what *should* be, but we can easily see what *shouldn't* be, and the pathway to this secret knowledge is suffering through alienation. For Marx, then, the Absolute isn't some ideal we can envision and manifest; it's what's left over when all the evil of the world is driven away. And what is that? All that exists.

Marx's Gnostic leanings were stronger than Hegel's, in other words, and he saw the world constructed by the bourgeois classes of society—the *bürgerliche Gesellschaft*—as a prison created by (some) men for Man. That is, Marxism is a recreation of ancient Gnosticism with the bourgeoisie taking the place of the incarcerating demon called the Demiurge, which is the "artisan" being that constructs the world so that it imprisons the spiritual essence of Man. Marxism is revolutionary Sociological Gnosticism—Gnosticism in which the spiritual world is social rather than transcendent—with the bourgeoisie constructing all of social reality to alienate Man from his true self, which he would come to know through his work if that weren't being expropriated into someone else's profit in exchange for wages, and to imprison him in exploitative conditions. This suffering confers a secret, hidden, cult knowledge about our true natures: we're perfectly social (read: spiritual) beings who have been estranged from our true nature by dint of being incarcerated in the Prison of Being and its demiurgic false religion of capitalism, which must be abolished. We compete because we are Fallen. We fell because private property and individuality estrange us from who we really are.

As a theology, the Theology of Marxism is ultimately one of negative utopianism. It believes in a perfected (Absolutized) world and society, but the utopia cannot be described in positive terms. Instead, it's "not that" to basically everything. That is, the utopia is what emerges and blooms, to use the correct alchemical language, when everything that isn't Ideal is critiqued out of existence. Sometimes this sentiment is a bit obscure but unmistakable. "*Communism* as the *positive* transcendence of *private property* as *human self-estrangement*, and therefore as the real *appropriation* of the *human* essence by and for man; communism therefore as the complete return of man to himself as a *social* (i.e., human) being," Marx wrote in his *Economic and Philosophic Manuscripts* of 1844 (p. 96, emphasis in the original). Sometimes it's much more direct. "In this sense, negative thinking is by virtue of its own internal concepts 'positive': oriented toward, and comprehending a future which is 'contained' in the present," as Herbert Marcuse put it in *An Essay on Liberation* (p. 87). As observed before, the Absolute for Marx, as Hegel might have phrased it, is the total absence of anything that is distinct from the Absolute. Since Marxism is ultimately more Socially Gnostic than Hegel's speculative philosophy, though, any such thing is intrinsically oppressive to the enlightened Gnostic Elect of the Marxist system, who are called "Socialists," and therefore deserves to perish.

Tracking back to the theology, the Absolute cannot be

Absolute at all if it isn't actually *Absolute*, which means techni-
cally *nothing* can actually be distinct from the Absolute in the
first place. There can only be that which illegitimately sets itself
aside from the Absolute, for its own glory or benefit, as did the
Demiurge in the Gnostic myths. That explains Marx's use of the
phrasing "returning" to our true selves above. It also means there
are three kinds of people in the system outlined by Marx. There
are the Gnostic Elect of his system, the Socialists, who understand the saving truth that Man's true nature is as a perfectly
social being who lives for the whole species. They are the good
people, in fact the only people who are *people* at all. Then there
are the people who have bought into the illusory system per-
petrated by the bourgeoisie-as-demiurge, who have a false consciousness that must be awakened to Socialism and out of evil
bourgeois values. Finally, there are the bourgeoisie themselves,
who cannot be awakened to Socialism because it is the human
truth of Socialism they seek to hide in the first place, and they are
wholly evil and must be utterly destroyed.

Much more could be said about this esoteric and wholly
evil theology. It is sufficient for the present to underscore that
Socialism is the name of the secret, hidden, salvific self-knowledge that can set Man free from the Prison of Being constructed
through all of political economic life by the demiurgic bourgeoisie. Class consciousness is the name for the first initial steps
toward a full Gnostic awakening to Socialism, his first awakening to the class structure and Gnostic alienation of society as
constructed by the bourgeoisie. As awakened Socialists, Man
knows himself as himself: as a fully social being who creates and
eventually completes and humanizes his whole world, himself,
and others such that he sees in it only himself and his realized life
activity, his work. Since nothing can exist outside of the Absolute
in this theology, Man must take the world *and himself* as his

object and fully "humanize" both, which is to say he must transform it by "doing the work" that makes all of Man communist ("inclusive") and all of Nature remade to be fit for Socialist Man ("sustainable"). So Marxism is a Gnostic-Hermetic mystery religion posing as economics, politics, and sociology that holds that all distinctions from its own cult beliefs about reality are at best illusions and at worst deliberate evil that, in either case, must be obliterated and transformed into compliance—*aufheben*.

The people in this lineage, writ large, are Social Gnostics. Different Social Gnostics view the alienating and incarcerating Social Demiurge, who controls the "means of production" of Man, differently. Marx saw economic conditions as deterministic and historical, because for him the idea of private property necessitates individualism, which is what distinguishes one person from another and maintains the "bourgeois" carceral illusion that prevents Socialism. His solution: *abolish private property*. Other types of Social Gnostics choose other societal "systems" as demiurgic. Critical Race Theory chooses the imposition of racial categories, allegedly by white people, as structurally deterministic through access to the form of bourgeois cultural property called "whiteness." Its Elect are "antiracists," and their goal is to achieve "racial justice" by abolishing whiteness. As I documented at length in *Race Marxism* in 2022, it's the same program: Sociological Gnosticism.

In this volume, Queer Marxism is presented as regarding *normalcy* as a form of bourgeois private property that Queer Theory and Queer Activism are meant to abolish in order to liberate "queers" from the Prison of Being. It also points out that under the cult doctrine of Queer Theory, we're all queer, even if we don't know it. Queerness is an elevated but primordial state for us to awaken and *return* to. This is no different than the way Marx believed we are all essentially Socialist, although bourgeois illusions have obscured this fact, willfully or not, from us. In Queer Theory, it is the socially constructed illusion of *normalcy* that hides our queer natures and prevents our emancipation from social-spiritual prison. Though outside the scope of this work, Critical Race Theory is precisely the same program under the belief that the imposition of socially meaningful racial categories (by whites onto "people of color") is the demiurgic problem.

"Queer" then, isn't an identity. It isn't even a political stance, though that's how it's practiced and described. It is a state of Social Gnostic awakening in a relentlessly destructive cult that just so happens to be utterly and completely obsessed with not just sex, but *deviant sex*. For reasons that are probably pretty profound to human psychological and social development, this makes the primary mission field of this cult religion be *our children*, and that's what this plainspoken volume is meant to reveal.

The tactic of targeting children isn't just perverse; it's also manipulatively demonic. Most adults, even with their empathy weaponized, are little susceptible to the Queer Gnostic cult. Even sexual minorities, once granted civil rights and social acceptance within the *normal* variations of human experience, are difficult to radicalize into something as toxic and acidic as Queer Gnosticism—which is demonstrably to the Queer Activists' chagrin. Children, however, are much easier to manipulate and, in fact, to break, and adults *love their children*. Adults who adopt the Queer Gnostic cult very frequently do either in a desperate attempt to prove their inclusive virtue or, far more often, in allyship with a sexual or "gender" minority relative or friend, usually a child, niece, nephew, or some other close relation. The initiated child is the gateway to the social-emotional initiation of the adults in their lives, who have their love weaponized into the twisted value called "inclusion."

Sickeningly, this "relationship allyship" is problematic to

all of the "Woke" Gnostic sects. It isn't adequate to care about "queer" issues just because you know and love someone who is Gnostically queer. That's *selfish*. It's *self-serving*. It upholds the distinction between you and yours and the collective many. You must have *better* reasons for your support. You must *become queer* yourself. Your initiation through your loved ones is merely an entry point to relentless emotional and psychological abuse meant to trap you in the cult forever. Once you make costly sacrifices, like your child's physical integrity and future health and fecundity, they have almost always got you. Of course, it still won't be good enough, and, as the psychology and sociology of these situations tend to play out, you will atone for this shame by advocating relentlessly and viciously for the cult and its expansion, especially to other children to perpetuate the cycle. You can see these people demonstrating in bright rainbow colors outside any meeting in America or Canada today that dares stand up for parental rights, for example. The snake eating its own tail is, in fact, the cycle of abuse.

Just like how the esoteric religions behind this cult aren't new, neither are the cult's mob behaviors. All of these practices are attendant throughout Gnostic totalitarian cults, whether Puritan, Jacobin, Communist, Nazi, Fascist, Islamist, or any other. Crucially to our American and Western contexts, they were specifically honed in Communist China in the 1950s and 1960s by Mao Zedong and his CCP. Mao's "thought reform" (literally, brainwashing) campaigns primarily targeted youth, weaponized internalized shame, and made use of two readily familiar weapons we see today, including in Queer Theory.

The first of Mao's great tools was his transformational "formula," which he called "unity, criticism, unity." Today, we might call it "belonging, problematizing, and inclusion." Mao said you start with a desire for unity, then criticize and struggle those elements who prevent the desired unity because of their incorrect values, and then arrive at a new unity on a new basis, which he named "socialist discipline." In other words, you tell the people that everyone wants to get along, creating a strong social pressure to conform, and then you set contrived terms upon which "getting along" counts. Those terms define the "new unity on a new basis." In even clearer words, narcissistic abusers establish the terms of a cult and insist they'll cause trouble for everyone until everyone gets on board. Just like the slogan "no justice, no peace" says, there will be no unity (no peace) until it's on the contrived terms of the "new basis" (justice). Everyone who is against the new basis (social justice) is therefore the impediment to unity and must be criticized and struggled for holding up the program.

For Mao, it was his great Socialist revolution and, in fact, his own religion of Mao-worship. Today, it's almost the same. We start with a desire for a new unity on a new basis: "We just want a place where everyone feels like they belong." Belonging, though, is defined in terms of Woke "inclusion," which means including only those who have a Woke consciousness and only that which coddles their Woke sensibilities. Everything else is "unsafe," "traumatizing," "marginalizing," or "oppressive," say "racist," "sexist," "homophobic," "ableist," "transphobic," or whatever. So everyone who doesn't want to have "inclusive values," which is a new basis upon which the new unity of "belonging" will stand, has to be criticized and struggled until they adopt the right values or are purged from the system. In Queer Activism, then, everyone who fails to "affirm" and "celebrate" whatever it is that the Queer Activists and their initiated acolytes demand, is problematically homophobic, transphobic, or something, and has to be criticized, struggled, shamed, censored, and purged. It's the exact same formula. The only difference is that each queered person is to worship themselves *as queer* rather than worshiping the centralized character of Mao Zedong (whom many of them revere nonetheless).

Mao also weaponized identity politics, classifying the people who were in his cult as having good identities, which he coded "red," and those who were against his cult as having bad identities, which he coded "black." Black identities were not considered people. They were *enemies of the people*, and Mao's programming relentlessly taught the people to *hate* the enemies of the people, who were holding up any possibility of unity under socialist discipline. Because, as it is said, the Iron Law of Woke Projection never misses, in our day, the people who hold up the possibility of a new unity under sustainability and inclusion are said to be participating in… *hate*.

Mao's identity politics system deserves an entire chapter to elaborate on how exquisitely evil it is and then another to show philosophically and historically how "intersectionality" in our day is the Western adaptation of that same program to the American sociopolitical context, but a shorter description will have to suffice. In the very shortest expression, Mao defined a variety (initially five) of "black" identities that were bad: landlord, rich farmers, "bad elements," counterrevolutionaries, and right-wing extremists—at least a couple of which readers in the West today will find haunting, though "conspiracy theorist," "domestic extremists," and "basket of deplorables" might be more familiar wording. These identities were contagious. If you had them, you could give them to others, usually family members automatically. That is, Mao created the first social credit system.

He outlined in contrast five "red" identities among "the people": laborer (hammer), peasant (sickle), revolutionary soldiers, revolutionary cadres (or leaders), and revolutionary martyrs. That is, you could be in one of the token groups upheld by Communism and get some inclusion into the ranks of "the people," or you had to join the revolution explicitly and work for it. Anyone in a red category could lose that status at once if they were too closely associated with people with black identities, expressed the wrong views or values, or were turned in on suspicion of such from others in good standing. This encouraged rampant and backstabbing snitch culture, spying, and psychotic displays of loyalty and commitment to socialism, the CCP, and Mao because otherwise you would be thrown in prison or dragged into the public square to be humiliated and struggled, probably viciously, perhaps fatally.

Mao targeted youth with this program in his schools particularly, so much so that one of the easiest ways for a child to earn red-class status was to turn in a family member, parent, or teacher for counter-revolutionary or right-wing sentiments. This created a powerfully radicalized youth which coalesced violently in the mid-1960s into what was called the Red Guard, which destroyed property, people's lives, and people in a fervent mob that was held out as the true future of Communist China. They went virtually unopposed until Mao regained full power in 1967, after which he had them destroyed.

This system of identity politics was a powerful sociological radicalizing force in CCP-controlled China under Mao, and it is replicated by Woke Marxism, including Queer Theory and Queer Activism, here in the West today. The "black" categories are the "dominant groups" who have "privilege," probably along with landlords, whom the young people today really hate. The "red" categories are the Woke Gnostic categories of activists, including "queer," in the various domains of intersectional thought, together with other members of "marginalized groups" so long as they more or less keep quiet and keep their heads down. That is, the laborers and peasants of Woke Marxism are racial minorities, sexual minorities, the disabled, women (kind of, sometimes), and so on across the identity categories, so long as they are quiet little human shields for the radicals to hide behind. The revolutionary categories are the activists like in Antifa, BLM, Queer Activists, and so on, including allies (initiates) and "queer" people, who are distinct from sexual minorities by virtue of radicalization. Because skin color and other statuses are much harder to change, activists and "queer" are the easiest "red" categories to enter, and among these only queer cannot really be challenged or doubted. This creates a tremendous sociological pressure pump pushing kids into "queer identities," which is to say to join the Queer Gnostic cult.

Just to give you some idea of the parallelism, at least in Critical Race Theory, between this identity politics dynamic and Mao's, remember that under Mao, the only real pathway into a "red" identity was through taking up revolutionary leadership in some capacity. That is, you had to *become a revolutionary*. Further, that status was always contingent, so you had to continue "doing the work" to keep it. Now consider the Woke Gnostic status conferred under Critical Race Gnosticism: *anti-racist*. One of this cult's greatest purveyors is Robin DiAngelo, who taught untold millions of people to put themselves and others through "anti-racist" struggle sessions (brand name: "white fragility"). DiAngelo described being an anti-racist as a "lifelong commitment to an ongoing process" that includes "self-reflection, self-critique, and social activism." In other words, you have to "do the work," *for life*, while relentlessly putting yourself through a Maoist-style process of self-criticism and revolutionary leadership as an activist. Queer Activism is no different. The actualization of the Queer Marxist (or Queer Gnostic) cult in present-day America is simply part of Maoism with American characteristics.

What Queer Activism is building in our youth is not just broken generations of kids, physically, psychologically, and spiritually. It is also a highly radicalized youth contingent that fights for the Queer Marxist cult in specific and the Woke Marxist cult in general *all the time* as though it were a religious duty (which, for them, it is). That is, it's creating a *Rainbow Guard* that can be deployed against American society and the societies of other Western nations, their parents, their teachers, professionals, friends, and anyone else who the cult needs subdued by their radicalism. Isn't that what we see?

Mao radicalized the youth through the schools, particularly his revolutionary colleges, universities, and high schools, though brainwashing was standard throughout all grades under his entire reign. They became the Red Guard, got Mao his power back, and then were summarily discarded, just like Hegel said almost 150 years earlier: "History uses people and then discards them." The same process is happening in our schools throughout the West, especially in America and Canada. Queer Theory is one of the integral elements of that project and perhaps the most destructive. That's why this book by Logan Lancing is so timely and so valuable. That's why this fight matters so much, and that's why we have to understand what we're fighting so we can win it.

What we are witnessing is a cultural revolution in America. It is Maoism with American characteristics, and that implies that it is an ancient esoteric cult religion put into destructive practice so that it might save the world by destroying it completely. The vehicle for this evil project relies upon what is exposed and explained in this book: the queering of the American child. With our children, no matter what fight we put up, the cult gets the future—at least until everything collapses under its incompetence and grift. Without our children, all bets for them are off. It's our duty to stand for our kids and fight for their future. It's our responsibility to expose and end the influence of this cult. It's our mission to inform and empower our fellow citizens to take decisive action to preserve our society, protect our children, and recover our schools by expelling this cult from all aspects of public life and pushing it back to the thinnest margins, where it belongs. America's children shall not be queered, and their future will be bright and *normal*.

ACKNOWLEDGMENTS

This book wouldn't have been possible were it not for the narcissistic, self-serving "academics" (read: activists) who have worked tirelessly to put their mommy and daddy issues on full-display consistently, repeatedly, and at book length. Thank you for writing it all down. If not for your insatiable appetite for affirmation, I fear my readers would find the passages in this book too insane to be believed. I'll let them take you at your words.

The academy is lost. I couldn't turn to "the experts" for conversation while researching this book because the experts are frauds who no longer care about truth. Instead, I honed my ideas and arguments in concert with the thousands of strangers who are working tirelessly to expose the cult of Queer Theory (and Marxism). Thank you all for the impact you have had on me and your communities.

I can't overstate how influential the New Discourses Podcast and Dr. James Lindsay have been for me. The New Discourses podcast was often ground zero for my research, especially my investigations into the cult of Marxism (and Queer Marxism).

I'm happy to credit the best insights of this book to the jaw-dropping revelations found over at New Discourses.

Dr. Lindsay's insight and contributions make this book something much more than it was when I initially sent it to him. He has a brilliant mind, and it was a pleasure to work with him to provide you with the *truth* of Queer Theory.

Last but not least, this book wouldn't have been possible without my wife's patience and support. I told her that I needed to write this book when she was seven months pregnant with our second child. She asked me if it was important that I write it now. "Yes," I replied. "You do this every time," she said. I knew I had my answer.

www.ingramcontent.com/pod-product-compliance
Lightning Source LLC
Chambersburg PA
CBHW022048020426
42335CB00012B/594